A Relentless Threat

A Relentless Threat

Scholars Respond to Teens on Weaponized School Violence

Edited by

Kjersti VanSlyke-Briggs
Elizabeth A. Bloom

ROWMAN & LITTLEFIELD
Lanham • Boulder • New York • London

Published by Rowman & Littlefield
An imprint of The Rowman & Littlefield Publishing Group, Inc.
4501 Forbes Boulevard, Suite 200, Lanham, Maryland 20706
www.rowman.com

6 Tinworth Street, London, SE11 5AL, United Kingdom

Copyright © 2021 by Kjersti VanSlyke-Briggs and Elizabeth A. Bloom

All rights reserved. No part of this book may be reproduced in any form or by any electronic or mechanical means, including information storage and retrieval systems, without written permission from the publisher, except by a reviewer who may quote passages in a review.

British Library Cataloguing in Publication Information Available

Library of Congress Cataloging-in-Publication Data Available

ISBN 9781475857665 (cloth : alk. paper) | ISBN 9781475857672 (pbk. : alk. paper) | ISBN 9781475857689 (epub)

∞™ The paper used in this publication meets the minimum requirements of American National Standard for Information Sciences—Permanence of Paper for Printed Library Materials, ANSI/NISO Z39.48-1992.

Contents

Introduction: Where We Began ... ix
Elizabeth A. Bloom

Chapter 1: Challenges and Prospects for Policymaking to Address Gun Violence ... 1
Gina L. Keel

Chapter 2: Considering Ostracism Events as a Precursor to School Shootings ... 27
Fatima Albrehi and Lukas Pelliccio

Chapter 3: Evolving Boundaries: Bullying, Online Intimidations, and Social Antagonisms ... 47
Brian M. Lowe

Chapter 4: What We Talk About When We Talk About School Shootings: Framing the Stoneman Douglas High School Shooting in the Twitterverse ... 69
Ryan Ceresola

Chapter 5: Macabre Money: Capitalizing on School Shootings ... 89
Heather J. Matthews

Chapter 6: Sandy Hook Promise: Research Informed Practices ... 105
Rachel Masi and Justin E. Heinze

About the Editors and Contributors ... 119

"I was in the dark with my class—all under desks. I tried to compose my last text to my mom. We didn't know that it was a false alarm."—Lina, age 12

Introduction: Where We Began

Elizabeth A. Bloom

When much of the country shut down in the late winter 2020, sheltering in place for fear of contracting Covid-19, schools shuttered, and teachers and children pursued their teaching and learning from home. As winter turned to spring, a tweet, launched into the world by *Washington Post* reporter Robert Klemko on April 13, began making the rounds (@RobertKelmko). It proclaimed, "Last month was the first March without a school shooting since 2002." Though the accuracy of this statement was debatable, the underlying truth was undeniable; schools were closed and the killing had stopped.

Since the Columbine tragedy shocked the nation in 1999, the ever-present threat of weaponized violence in schools, perpetrated by teen shooters, has cast a pall over every person who crosses the threshold of an American school. Is today the day? Will it be my last? Will I be able to contact my mother? Will I have the courage to fight back?

When we began this project, we solicited statements from middle and high school students about how they experience the threat of a school shooting in their daily lives. Their poignant reflections reveal young people grappling with the meaning of safety, love, and their identities as heroes or cowards. As teacher educators and mothers, ourselves, we wondered whether perhaps this was the right time to launch a conversation about the reality that our children, students, colleagues, and partners in K–12 schools wrestle with every day.

This book represents the answer to that question and explores an educational landscape characterized by the imminent threat of weaponized school violence; where lockdown drills, "hardened" schools, and armed adults have become the norm. Efforts to effect policy change limiting access to firearms have fallen on a grassroots movement driven by those who have been most profoundly and tragically affected: the students and parents who have been its victims. All too often, without the power of their moneyed opponents, these ordinary citizen-advocates have been dismissed by elected officials as soon as the smoke clears from the latest shooting.

This volume provides a much-needed scholarly addition, from across disciplines, to understanding the problem of gun violence in U.S. schools. Our hope is to contribute to making common sense policy changes that reflect the will of the majority of Americans, and to stand in solidarity with the often-marginalized voices of grassroots activists.

As we undertook this project, we invited scholars from across a variety of disciplines to respond directly to the voices of students and teachers. We wanted to represent a variety of perspectives to explore the multifaceted complexities of the phenomenon of weaponized school violence. We asked our authors to choose and then respond to one of the personal statements that we had collected from students in grades 7–12. Each chapter begins and is written in response to the raw, unvarnished voices of young people who we have collectively failed to keep safe.

We begin this volume by contextualizing the tragic specter of deadly weaponized attacks in our public schools. In her chapter, *Challenges and Prospects for Policymaking to Address Gun Violence,* Gina L. Keel introduces the reader to the social and political contexts for policymaking in the halls of government, by providing an overview of the sometimes interlocking and conflicting influences of diverse activist constituencies, cultural forces, and institutional systems. Her comprehensive historical outline situates the current debate over gun rights policy and adds critical depth to our understanding of the sources of inertia that prevent substantive change from being enacted.

Given that, according to a recent Gallup poll, a bipartisan majority of Americans support some restrictions on citizens' access to guns, Keel provides a clear explanation for how it can be that we haven't gotten there yet (https://news.gallup.com/poll/1645/guns.aspx). She identifies gun violence as a "wicked problem" (i.e., what policy studies scholars describe as a social problem characterized by failure to reach consensus, even on its definition, and a consequent inability to develop, win support for, and implement policy to mitigate it).

Gun violence in the U.S. is especially wicked according to Keel because, as the history of gun control versus gun rights politics will show, it pits grassroots citizens with a powerfully compelling argument against a well-funded opponent deeply connected to the levers of political power. Like other social problems we face in the United States today, the solutions are hidden behind layers of obfuscation, manipulation, and posturing by our leaders.

Keel's macro level discussion is followed by a chapter by Fatima Albrehi and Lukas Pelliccio who consider the intimate circumstances from which three teen shooters emerged and then examine the analogous factors that triggered each of their attacks. In *Considering Ostracism Events as Precursors to School Shootings*, Albrehi and Pelliccio examine three cases in which the perpetrators were subjected to ostracism, specifically romantic rejection, which catalyzed their decisions to exact vengeance on their victims. The authors provide a more nuanced analysis that complicates the familiar narratives on which media and policy makers generally focus, including access to firearms, mental illness, and bullying as the causes weaponized school violence.

Albrehi and Pelliccio propose that ostracism, a very specific type of bullying, in which individuals are unintentionally or purposefully ignored or shunned, can act as a devastating precipitating factor to acts of violence by teenage boys. Until now, the idea of ostracism as a catalyst has invited little attention among the public and has therefore been ignored in programs and policies aimed at prevention. With a more nuanced understanding of the phenomenon, strategies for targeting and then preventing root causes might be developed.

Brian M. Lowe frames his chapter, *Evolving Boundaries: Bullying, Online Intimidations and Social Antagonisms* by chronicling the historical evolution of bullying in the U.S. from face-to-face exchanges between people who know each other to online exchanges between strangers. Lowe demonstrates, via several case studies, how the traditional definition of adolescent bullying, what Lowe call the, "Traditional Ideal Type," acts as a mechanism for maintaining social status hierarchies among teens.

In Traditional Ideal Type bullying, victims may be subjected to verbal, symbolic or physical exchanges that either occur in physical proximity or through other hostile communication. This type of bullying generally transpires within the confines of the school campus and is therefore subject to adult supervision, albeit limited, when it occurs in liminal spaces like the hallway or locker room. There is also a degree of reassurance and predictability when bullying occurs in school. School community members understand that deviant behavior will be identified, categorized and punished according to the degree of its severity by adults who are the ultimate arbiters of social control. Further, he suggests that Traditional Type bullying may serve a social purpose in our culture as it reflects similar patterns in adult social interactions.

The omnipresence of social media in the lives of today's young people has radically transformed their social landscape in ways that adults are only beginning to understand. In contrast to the Traditional Type, Lowe illuminates the profound expansion in social boundaries in online communication and explores what social purposes it might serve, particularly among boys. Online bullying appears to exist on a continuum from bonding as boys "trash talk" each other as they engage in video gaming, to vicious taunting and threats from anonymous tormentors.

Online bullying is significantly more insidious than traditional bullying; there's no escape for the victim, he is helpless to retaliate or explain it to himself because it is often anonymous, it can devolve into extreme and relentless cruelty, and the bullies themselves are not constrained by adult surveillance. Because of its covert nature, it is harder to study online bullying and therefore harder to mitigate. Lowe addresses this gap in our understanding by mapping the online lives of several teens who made the ultimate choice to kill.

While Lowe examines the broad sweep of social media's power and influence among teens, Ryan Ceresola concentrates on one facet, the microblogging juggernaut of Twitter. In *What We Talk About When We Talk About School Shootings: Framing the Stoneman Douglas High School Shooting in the Twitterverse,* Ceresola examines the way that the subject of gun violence is framed in real time by people using the digital platform Twitter and does an analysis of how public opinion is shaped and swayed in this virtual community. Ceresola focuses on the digital aftermath of one tragic incident, the killings at Marjory Stoneman Douglas High School, to identify the competing or complimentary themes in the Twitterverse.

While tweets are issued in bite-sized packages with a 280-character limit, they can be enormously consequential as the writer with the most followers and retweets can influence public opinion which, in turn, can drive policy initiatives. Ceresola explains that understanding the way public perception of the causes and solutions to gun violence can be better understood by analyzing the way it unfolds in real time on Twitter. This understanding can then be used by advocates for common sense gun control for framing their arguments in such a way as to more effectively sway public opinion and therefore impact policy decisions.

Commercial incentives are the focus of Heather J. Matthews's chapter, *Macabre Money: Capitalizing on School Shootings.* She begins with a brief recounting of her experience teaching in a rural school with a culture where deer and turkey hunting are beloved traditions. As in many similar American communities, guns are regarded as tools for sustenance, bonding among friends and family, and fostering ties to the land. Matthews notes that she did not question the omnipresence of guns in her students' lives until the shooting at Marjorie Stoneman Douglas High School in 2018.

With an anxiety that began to consume her, Matthews became fixated on researching the purchasing of safety gear, which subsequently led to her dawning awareness of the macabre profit to be made from fear generated by the gruesome regularity of school shootings across the country. Her search led her to discover a truly astounding $2.7 billion industry that preys and capitalizes on the distress and worry of parents, teachers, and school districts alike, selling snake oil, to unwitting customers desperate for a sense of agency. She exposes the reader to a lucrative market, not just for items that promise security, from smoke bombs to hallway cannons, but also for trainings, conferences, and workshops.

While investing in the hardening of schools may appear as responsible action, it actually distracts our attention from taking steps that may prevent violence in the first place. Matthews does not advocate excluding all such measures, but calls for a more balanced approach that puts addressing root causes, emphasizing student well-being, and exercising the power of the vote at the forefront.

There is a truism passed around among teachers that policy makers get swept up, bringing teachers with them, by educational interventions that promise educational remedies to social problems. Any veteran teacher can catalog examples of programs, which appeared to be implemented on a whim and enforced with urgency, only to be tossed out without a serious evaluation before moving on to the next shiny thing. Conversely, Rachel Masi and Justin Heinz advocate for effective and sustainable solutions for the long term to the problem of weaponized school violence. Their efforts to prevent school violence are firmly grounded in evidence-based research, and include partnership with all stakeholders to ensure a mutual sense of ownership.

In their chapter, *Research Informed Solutions through Practice and Partnerships,* Masi and Heinze claim that our current practices focus on reactions to violent episodes, while they focus on prevention. They represent Sandy Hook Promise (SHP) which is a nationally recognized grassroots nonprofit organization built and led by families and loved ones of the victims of the mass killing that occurred at Sandy Hook Elementary School in Newtown, Connecticut on December 14, 2012.

Their mission is to end school shootings by setting a culture change in motion that empowers students and school personnel to stop violence before it happens. Sandy Hook Promise partnered with the University of Michigan to create the Know the Signs Programs including Start with Hello, Say Something, and the Say Something Anonymous Reporting System. Their partnership serves as a practical model that schools and school districts can emulate for a safer future for all.

Research has shown that successful programs and initiatives that are characterized by a multipronged approach that includes strengthening community connectedness, offering high quality mental and physical health services, prioritizing the importance healthy relationships between students and staff, and investing in safe and stable communities. However, this approach is not a proscription. Masi and Heinze contend that because each community is different, imposing a one-size-fits-all program, diminishes the likelihood of its long-term success. Sandy Hook Promise emphasizes that it is imperative to do both a needs assessment study that includes all stakeholders and a survey of resources before a prevention program is implemented.

The research represented here in *A Relentless Threat: Scholars Respond to Teens on Weaponized School Violence* is important for several reasons. It is time that Americans face up to the phenomenon of weaponized school violence as a uniquely American phenomenon among our western counterparts. The U.S. far outranks any of our first world counterparts in the frequency and lethality of gun violence committed on school grounds (https://worldpopulationreview.com/country-rankings/school-shootings-by-country). The number of deaths that we endure, including suicides and those where the victims were targeted, is staggering.

It is tempting to look to other countries for direction. In Australia in 1996, for example, a twenty-eight-year-old with a semi-automatic weapon gunned down 35 people in the town of Port Arthur, Australia. The government response was swift and decisive. Hundreds of thousands of firearms were turned in by citizens in a national buyback program, long waiting periods for gun purchases were instituted, buyers were required to submit reasons for purchase excluding personal safety, semi-automatic and automatic weapons were banned and finally, heavy fines and even prison sentences were meted out to those who refused to comply. With only a few exceptions, Australians have been almost entirely free from the scourge of lethal gun violence since.

Unfortunately, using Australia as a model is ineffective as our history and cultures differ in significant ways. One feature of American culture that bears scrutiny is our veneration of individualism as a preeminent social value and our denial of the ways it poisons other realms of our national culture. If any phenomenon could illustrate the malignancy of elevating extreme individualism to a social good, it would be the refusal of large swathes of the U.S. population to wear face masks to protect others during the devastating Covid-19 pandemic of 2020. As one angry citizen declaimed in a video that he posted on his Twitter account after refusing to put on a mask, "I'm not doin' it 'cause when I woke up this morning I was in a free country."

The gun debate mirrors other conflicts that bedevil our society, individual freedom trumps all other values. We should consider emphasizing civic duty, communitarianism, and mutual empathy in our school curricula. Without it we risk the emotional health of our children. The personal trauma and anxiety that manifests as a result of the constant threat of violence is real; we explore these issues in depth our second book, *Dress Rehearsals for Gun Violence: Confronting Trauma and Anxiety in America's Schools.*

Our culture is in an accelerating state of crisis as economic uncertainty, climate change, political divisiveness, racial strife, and an unstoppable pandemic threaten to engulf us. While American history is marked by protracted periods of violence and polarization, the present day seems particularly ominous. Children watch their parents and absorb their attitudes, beliefs, and values. They see that our culture is weaponized in general, and they see the heightened aggression and anger in the adults in their lives.

Schools, as we know them, are still on a hiatus from their normal functioning, but sooner or later when the virus subsides, we wonder whether the pestilence of increased hostility and toxic division that we absorb all around us will seep ever deeper into the schools our children inhabit. It is imperative that Americans recognize that we will reap what we have sown. The pandemic has afforded us protracted moment to reflect on our children's future; let us use it to reconsider what we want it to be.

Chapter 1

Challenges and Prospects for Policymaking to Address Gun Violence

Gina L. Keel

> "I think adults need to know that school shootings are complex and intertwined in every aspect of our lives. For many it was the catalyst for political involvement, so it feels hurtful when the issue is minimized and generalized. It's especially hurtful when we're told to stay out of politics that we're 'too young' to understand, because sadly we understand this issue better than many adults ever will."—Angel, age 17

Gun violence is a complex, multidimensional problem that involves legal and illegal access and use of various types of firearms in ways that harm and endanger individuals, families, and social groupings—at schools, churches, concerts, and more. "More than 19,500 people were victims of homicide and over 47,000 people died by suicide in 2017 alone," according to the Centers for Disease Control's (CDC's) *National Violent Death Reporting System*. Homicides and suicides have increased since 2015 to levels not seen since the 1990s, and almost half of all Americans say they know someone who has been shot, whether accidental or intentional (Gramlich & Schaeffer, 2019).

Mass shootings, including those at schools, account for far less than 1% of firearm deaths, but they have increased alarmingly in the past decade. Federal Bureau of Investigation (FBI) studies of "active shooter incidents" show the average number of incidents rising from just over six per year in the early aughts to more than 20 per year since 2014 (Gramlich, 2019). Survivors, families, and communities struggle with questions of why and what to do about gun violence. How do we address complex problems such as gun violence, which have such dire consequences? Who makes policy to address gun violence and what factors influence their decisions?

To answer these questions from a political science perspective, I examine the social and political context of gun policymaking in the U.S., including activism, culture, and institutions, and then turn to the perspectives of policy experts who seek to inform policy decisions with fact-based analyses. Experts in public health, academia, and think tanks estimate risks of gun violence and evaluate how particular gun rights, regulations, and laws impact gun violence, including mass shootings, domestic violence, and suicides that affect youth.

Policy approaches to violence include preventive, policing, and hardening strategies that also apply to school settings, for example restricting access of persons and places and limiting types of weapons. No other developed country has gun violence as great as the U.S. The firearm homicide rate is approximately 25 times higher than other high-income countries based on World Health Organization data, so it is important to also consider gun culture and policies from a comparative perspective (Grinshteyn & Hemenway, 2016, p. 267).

THE POLITICS OF GUN RIGHTS VERSUS GUN CONTROL

In democratic political systems, including the United States, one can expect and should respect civic engagement by diverse groups via protests, social and other media expression, and lobbying for influence. When large numbers of people mobilize for change, to up-end an intolerable status quo and achieve a new order, it is identified as a social movement (Tarrow, 1998).

Movements can emerge and grow in response to triggering events and inspired leadership that expand debates and the number of adherents, but movements also require resources and opportunities to influence policymaking. Organized private interests, and grassroots pressures from constituents can influence decisions of policymakers, but ideology and partisanship have created political boundaries for what is possible in the U.S.

The late 1970s ushered in conservative antiregulatory politics, especially in the U.S., and provided an opportunity for social and political action in response to high violent crime rates and economic anxiety. Gun rights activists organized to limit government authority for regulating firearms and secure individual rights to purchase and use weapons for self and property defense and crime deterrence. Activists remade the National Rifle Association (NRA) into one of the most politically powerful interest groups in history with nearly five million dues-paying members. For nearly 100 years, the NRA was an organization for sporting and hunting enthusiasts that had supported some gun control measures but in the mid-1970s shifted its mission and motto to the broad promotion of gun rights and purported defense of the Second Amendment.

The NRA became overtly political despite its legal status as a 501(c)(4) charitable organization and was the key organization in the gun rights movement (Lepore, 2012). It created an institute for legislative action, funded revisionist legal scholarship on the 2nd Amendment, and endorsed a presidential candidate (Reagan) for the first time. The group secured a politicized congressional investigation into the origins of the Second Amendment, and lobbied Congress to weaken the 1968 Gun Control Act's restrictions on military surplus firearms.

The NRA recruited members and mobilized to them to become vocal gun rights advocates and voters. Its membership grew large. Their promotion of gun rights and "apocalyptic predictions about the threat of gun confiscation and domestic disarmament" (Cornell & Kozuskanich, 2013, p. 4) may have contributed to an increase in gun ownership and volume of guns purchased. Today, based on Pew Research polling, approximately 30% of Americans personally own a gun, most of them have multiple guns, and two-thirds say "protection" is the main reason. Hunting and sporting is a lesser reason, except to rural owners (Gramlich & Schaeffer, 2019).

The NRA promotes local firearms trainings and "activist centers" to engage members and gives material benefits including national magazines, equipment discounts, and accident insurance, while monetizing membership for tens of millions of dollars in dues, advertising fees and product endorsements. Their organizational strategy is "offering benefits and services that build deep and lasting relationships with members, and then activating those members for long-term, systemic change goals" (Murray, 2013, p. 34).

The NRA today exerts pressure on candidates to support their gun rights agenda and block gun control initiatives by leveraging campaign contributions and outside election spending, rating elected officials' performance on gun rights issues, and keeping their members attuned through various media platforms. Gun rights activists invoke a policy argument of "more guns, less crime" (Lott, 1998) and push for expansion of firearm freedoms to broadly "acquire, possess, collect, exhibit, transport, carry, transfer ownership of, and enjoy the right to use arms" according to the NRA mission statement. Gun advocates won rights-based laws including "concealed carry," adopted by 44 states since 1980, and Florida's Stand Your Ground law (2005), which protects deadly force in a confrontation (Lepore, 2012, p. 3).

Traditional conservatives, who support government power to curb social freedom and promote "family values," express skepticism of policy solutions to complex social problems including gun violence. They have supported the NRA and its gun freedom agenda.

Republican Party leaders, conservatives and activists, in Congress and in the executive branch generally favor promoting rather than regulating economic activity, including gun manufacturing and sale. They push back on calls for stricter controls or universal background checks, with antigovernment rhetoric.

Responding to the AME Baptist Church massacre by a young white supremacist, Senate Judiciary Chair Grassley (R-IA) emphasized a "bureaucratic mistake prevented existing laws from working" and criticized advocates using "tragedy to enact unnecessary gun laws" (Schmidt, 2015). In 1996, the Republican-controlled Congress passed the Dickey Amendment preventing the CDC from spending "to advocate or promote gun control" and cutting their budget, which chilled gun violence research that might arrive at conclusions supporting firearm regulation. In 2018, Congress clarified that the advocacy ban did not apply to research and has begun to modestly fund it.

Contemporary gun control activism has roots in the 1981 attempted assassination of President Reagan and shooting of his press secretary Jim Brady. Surviving serious brain injury, Brady and his wife led a national campaign to stop handgun sales to dangerous people. After a decade of lobbying and organizing local chapters, the Brady Handgun Violence Prevention Act was passed by the Democratic-controlled Congress and signed by newly elected President Clinton. This law required federal background checks on people who buy guns from *licensed dealers* to prevent sales to violent felons and people otherwise disqualified under state and federal laws.

Congress passed a federal assault weapons ban in 1994, but with a sunset provision. The ban prohibited manufacture for civilian use of semi-automatic firearms defined as assault weapons and large capacity ammunition magazines, but only as applied to newly manufactured guns. Existing guns were not restricted. The law was vigorously contested for how it defined weapon characteristics and whether it was effective in reducing violence (Cook & Goss, 2014, pp. 142–143; Koper, 2013).

Subsequent congresses did not reauthorize the law and it expired in 2004. Congress also passed the Violence Against Women Act in 1994, which included restrictions on firearm possession by those with protection orders against them. This law was also highly contested as too punitive, restricting rights based on potential threats, and for administrative difficulty given its reliance on state and local policing (Cook & Goss, 2014, pp. 145–146). These control laws were only possible because of interest group pressure, unified Democratic control of government 1992–1994, and a few moderate Republicans in the Senate who supported the legislation.

Democratic Party leaders, including President Clinton, long blamed their 1994 loss of the House and Senate control on backlash to their gun control legislation. These electoral losses created wariness for pursuing future gun control measures for more than a decade, as well as effectually creating an institutional veto when Republicans controlled either legislative chamber.

Women have been prominent in gun violence lobbying and public activism that included "Million Mom" marches. Their concerns for child safety drove organizing efforts, and most gun control groups active in 1990s were "created in direct response to a shooting involving one or more youths" (Goss, 2012, p. 2). The Columbine High School mass shooting (1999), a premeditated and brazen attack by two students who killed 12 students and one teacher, expanded the gun violence problem to schools, places formerly perceived as safe.

School shootings became a horror that shook all parents and touched an innate drive to protect their children. Complicating the goal of child safety, teenagers had become perpetrators as well as victims of gun violence, and not just in urban settings. Ultimately, calls for addressing gun violence has come from youth advocating for their own safety.

In recent years, youth leaders have emerged in the debates over gun violence in cities and schools, catalyzed by their personal experiences with seemingly random mass shooting events and drug and gang violence in cities such as Chicago. Young activists joined in the efforts of groups including Americans for Responsible Solutions, Sandy Hook Promise, Everytown for Gun Safety, and Moms Demand Action.

Following the February 2018 mass shooting at their high school in Parkland, Florida, student leaders Emma González and David Hogg and others became articulate spokespersons demanding action. By mobilizing school-aged kids and their allies in "March for Our Lives" events across the country, media-savvy youth leaders gained wide media coverage and pushed new firearm regulations onto the political agendas of several states including Republican-controlled Florida.

These anti-gun violence demonstrations were more inclusive than past efforts, elevating the profile of African American activists and groups such as Chicago's Project Orange Tree founded by teens after the 2013 shooting death of Hadiya Pendleton, who had just performed at President Obama's 2nd inaugural parade. The group is now part of the "Wear Orange" coalition of organizations, brands, and influencers to curb gun violence. The anti-gun violence youth movement has intersected with the Black Lives Matter movement for racial justice and policing reform, enlarging the debate and diversity of voices for change.

Researchers at the Center for American Progress concluded, "these young people do not just want to reform gun laws—they are also demanding that the issue of gun violence be examined as part of a complex and intersectional web of issues that also include community disinvestment, criminal justice reform, and policing" (Parsons et al., 2018, para. 5).

The new movement was successful in opening policy windows because of broad public support for action and regular media coverage. Public opinion in support for new gun control measures has increased to a clear majority. According to Pew Research polling, public support for stricter gun laws increased from 52% in 2017 to 60% in 2019, while support for less strict gun laws dropped from 18% to 11% (Schaeffer, 2019). Support for strengthening gun laws is even stronger among younger people, and it rose significantly after the Parkland Florida shooting. Harvard's Institute of Politics *Spring 2018 Youth Poll* found 64% of 18- to 29-year-olds favored stricter gun-control and 58 % favored a ban on assault weapons (Graphics 4 & 5).

Public outrage over mass shootings and parental fears about school safety have inspired policy responses by lawmakers, who are sensitive to constituents' demands and re-election pressures beyond the influence of the NRA. Since the 1999 Columbine attack, lawmakers have regularly introduced bills to close loopholes allowing private sales without a background check, including at gun shows, but gun rights supporters mobilized to block state and national legislative efforts.

In 2007, Virginia Governor Tim Kaine had to use an executive order to close the state loophole that had allowed the Virginia Tech shooter to purchase semi-automatic handguns despite his history of severe mental illness and court order for treatment. Bipartisan legislation to strengthen the National Instant Criminal Background Check System (NICS) passed and was signed by President Bush in 2008, yet background checks are still not required for private sales. This is the only national gun control measure passed since 1994.

President Obama pushed Congress to pass a universal background check requirement to close the private sale loophole nationwide. Even with presidential leadership, this effort could not overcome partisan gridlock in Congress. In his last year in office, President Obama issued executive orders to strengthen NICS background checks—reporting requirements and administration, but they were short-lived. President Trump embraced a gun rights policy position and used executive authority to weaken mental health reporting requirements in early 2017.

Gun control has been difficult to sustain on political agendas, and scholars have questioned its status as a movement. Advocates have struggled to compete with gun rights activists because of low membership compared to the NRA, limited funding from philanthropies, narrowly focused women's organizations, and weak narrative strategies (Goss, 2006; Goss 2012). The expansion of activism to include youth and racial justice groups may have reinvigorated the possibility for the gun control movement "by redefining the issues at stake in a way that passive sympathizers see it in their immediate self-interest to become actively involved in the political fray" (Goss, 2006, p. 105).

Restricting semi-automatic guns and high-capacity magazine purchases became a priority issue after several high-profile, high-casualty mass shootings and electoral shifts. Mass shootings at several schools (Virginia Tech, 2007, Sandy Hook Elementary, 2012, Marjorie Stoneman Douglas High, 2018) the hate-based nightclub attack (Orlando, 2016), and a sniper-style cascade of more than 1,000 rounds onto concert-goers (Las Vegas, 2017) increased calls for response to mass shootings at all levels of government.

Assailants in these and other incidents were able to legally purchase semi-automatic handguns, multiple firearms, and bump stocks to make rifles nearly fully automatic, despite their troubling histories with severe mental illness, domestic violence convictions, and even warnings by family and friends called in to their local police and the FBI. These incidents drew wide media attention and increased mobilization for gun control on social media platforms and in community demonstrations across the country.

States and local governments have responded to mass shootings and demands for action with a mix of policies limiting weapons, ammunition, and access, but also with enhanced security policies. The Giffords Law Center to Prevent Gun Violence (2020) attributes the 2019 passage of 70 gun-safety laws in 22 states and D.C. to widespread mobilization following the Marjory Stoneman Douglas High School shooting. This included a public safety act in Florida that banned "bump stocks" and raised the minimum age to purchase a firearm to 21.

The act also increased school security requirements, supported training for armed staff at schools, and gave law enforcement greater discretion to seize weapons from someone deemed mentally unfit. Other states adopted gun access restrictions, to protect victims of domestic violence, and permit-to-purchase laws.

Policymaking to address gun violence, particularly at the national level, remains nearly intractable despite mobilization for change and strong public support. Over 90% of Democrats and Republicans surveyed support "barring people with mental illnesses from purchasing guns," and majorities, with partisan differences, support banning high-capacity magazines and assault-style weapons (Schaeffer, 2019).

Movement politics, applying pressure to elected representatives, and cultivating public opinion are necessary but insufficient to secure gun control or gun rights legislation. Presidential and Congressional leadership with some bipartisan support will be required at the national level (Edwards et al., 1997, pp. 545, 561–562). Creating laws, regulations, or executive actions that conform to judicial rulings is also crucial in policy areas linked to Constitutional protections. These institutional challenges are exceptional in the United States.

GUN VIOLENCE AS A *WICKED PROBLEM*

Gun violence is among the most wicked problems in the United States because of "high levels of complexity, extreme uncertainty, and stakeholder disagreement to the point of paralysis" (Newman & Head, 2017, p. 43). The concept of a "wicked problem" in the parlance of policy studies refers to the inability to reach agreement on problem definition, develop and implement policy tools to mitigate the problem, and win support for the policy. Gun violence in the U.S. is particularly wicked because the nature of the complex problem is deeply contested by stakeholders, as shown by the history of gun rights versus gun control politics, and because rights and controls are unequal in practice.

Problem wickedness is also pronounced in the U.S. because of institutional fragmentation in the federal system, legal limitations, and administrative uncertainties that challenge positive actions. The stakeholder and institutional challenges are interwoven when local, state, and national governments struggle to pass and implement policies in polarized partisan environments. Political conflicts over proposals are magnified by uncertainty about the societal effects of policies and gun violence outcomes, even among expert policy analysts.

Uncertainty also plagues the question of whether and to what degree restrictions on gun purchases—weapon bans, background checks, and age restrictions—will reduce gun violence when an extraordinary number of guns are already in circulation. The *Small Arms Survey* is a reliable source to compare countries; the American firearm stockpile far exceeds every other large country. The survey lists over 393 million small firearms in civilian possession in the U.S., or 120.5 guns per 100 people, with only about one million of these arms registered (Karp, 2018, p. 4).

Background checks are not adequately reliable because they are not required for private sales and because of missing data and procedures. The NICS system completed 180 million background checks resulting in two million denials (1.5%) during 1998–2013 (Cook & Goss, 2014, p. 143). Yet several system lapses allowed purchases of AR-15-style rifles and semi-automatic handguns used in mass shootings, including Parkland, Florida, Sutherland Springs, Texas, and Blacksburg, Virginia.

Law enforcement and military agencies have failed to report domestic violence convictions, mental health orders, and even terror investigations. Even if a background check has not been completed, a licensed firearm dealer may deliver guns: "Following a delay decision, if the transaction is not resolved within the allowed three-business-day time frame, it is at the discretion of the FFL whether to transfer the firearm" (FBI, 2019).

The efficacy of state gun controls are also uncertain because of gun trafficking from less regulated into more regulated states, which is a sizable problem in New York and Illinois (Cook & Goss, 2014, pp. 139–140). State or national restrictions on types of weapons, such as the focus on assault rifles or ammunition magazine sizes, might also be undercut by assailants using semi-automatic handguns and multiple guns—the Las Vegas shooter, for example, had a stockpile in his hotel room (Kleck, 2009).

The unintended consequences of policy choices can be serious, including concerns for increased physical harms, discriminatory or arbitrary administration, and economic costs and trade-offs. Anticipation of new gun laws leads to spikes in gun purchases, as do poorly managed crises, which fuel fear.

Concealed carry laws can be written to require law enforcement to grant permits to eligible persons or written with a "may issue" provision that gives law enforcement discretion. This discretion may be misused against particular groups or persons. Resource-rich communities may be able or willing to invest in mental health access while more needy localities cannot or will not because of competing priorities. Focusing on school security and "target hardening" strategies through locks, video surveillance, locker searches, and lockdown drills can negatively affect the mental health of students and staff, particularly the youngest kids, and may infringe on their civil liberties (Addington, 2009, pp. 1436–1437; Warnick et al., 2018).

Stakeholder conflicts present social challenges to establishing gun policies because actors use moral claims, invoke individualistic political values, and tap into the exceptional American gun culture to oversimplify complex problems. Groups compete to define problems, frame issues, and shape policymaker and public opinions. Experiment-based research shows that public opinion is sensitive to how gun violence problems are framed, public safety versus individual rights for example, but "political predispositions" are intervening variables between information and opinion. Issue frames that reinforce existing partisan beliefs about causes of violence, blaming guns or blaming media violence for example, may contribute to political polarization that impedes policymaking (Haider-Markel & Joslyn, 2001).

Gun violence is not caused by one or two variables but advocates usually focus on people as the problem or guns as the problem in simplified ways that support their policy preferences for gun rights or gun control. Rights advocates promote policy to *increase legal access* to purchase and carry guns by focusing on individual rights of self-defense and property protection and by arguing that widespread gun ownership is a deterrent. They invoke foundational beliefs in American political philosophy of individual rights to life liberty and property, consent of the governed, and the role of government to protect rights, as found in the social contract theory of John Locke and articulated by Thomas Jefferson in the *Declaration of Independence*.

The gun violence problem is most often framed as "crime control" by gun rights advocates and focused on villainous perpetrators. Gun rights advocates often sensationalize threats by armed strangers, violent criminals and gangs in inner cities, or rare, random acts by mentally deranged individuals. The NRA is noted for using "alarmist rhetoric" to mobilize members and for responding to mass shooting events by calling for "more good guys with guns" to solve a perceived lack of security in schools (Spitzer, 2021, p.143, Merry, 2016, p. 382).

Rights advocates minimize concerns about gun prevalence and cross-border weapons flows; they prefer interdiction and heavily arming local police forces to respond. Their policy approach of arming more people to deter and defend against gun violence are based on fantastic claims and anecdotes rather than evidence.

In contrast, gun control advocates frame guns as inherently dangerous and increasingly lethal due to technological advances that enable rapid, mass casualties. A study of policy narratives by gun policy organizations, using Twitter data, found that the Brady Campaign emphasized innocent victims after the Sandy Hook school shooting. They invoked a moral mandate to take action supported by public support for "sensible reforms" and portrayed the gun lobby and politicians as "villains seeking to obstruct change" (Merry, 2016, p. 381). By focusing on preventable mass shootings and homicide victims, they advocate policies to *limit sale and access* to guns.

Gun control advocates use public health and crime statistical evidence more than rights groups do (Merry, 2016, p. 383). They argue that existing gun restrictions are inadequate to protect vulnerable people and that the effectiveness of existing controls is undermined by vast and numerous loopholes.

CULTURAL AND INSTITUTIONAL FACTORS

The sociopolitical context for crafting policy responses to gun violence is more wicked in the U.S. than in other western democracies because of our unique gun culture and structures of power. Political values of liberty and individualism are particularly strong and enshrined in the Bill of Rights, giving philosophical and legal advantages to gun rights positions. The European tradition of a gentlemen's privilege to bear arms was not planted in the colonies (Kennett & Anderson, 1975, p. 44). American gun culture—attitudes, practices, and mythology—is rooted in revolutionary and western settlement experiences and the myth of the frontier.

The power of myths is their "symbolizing function," which become part of a cultural language with deeply encoded metaphors and lessons learned from history (Slotkin, 1985, p. 16). Firearm myths, metaphors, and lessons are invoked in policy debates and can overwhelm arguments about complex, fact-based histories of gun regulation or contemporary needs. This helps explain why the "United States is the only modern industrial urban nation that persists in maintaining a gun culture" (Hofstadter, 1970, para.1).

Historians have demonstrated the strong role that colonial, state, and national governments played in regulating firearms. In the early period, the prevalence of citizen soldiers in colonial militias was necessitated by limited resources and participation was required. Military-style weapons were promoted but also controlled with storage and gunpowder regulations and restrictions on discharges; firearm possession was actively restricted to "citizens judged to be virtuous and loyal" (Cornell & Kozuskanich, 2013, p. 5). The symbolic power of beliefs about the virtue of citizen militias has persisted long after their rejection and replacement by professional, trained federal troops, national guards in states, and local police forces (Kennett & Anderson, 1975, p. 58).

Contemporary cultural attachment to guns is strongest among hunting and sporting enthusiasts, a shrinking portion of the population, and people who identify with a "militia/frontier ethos" believing that guns tamed the west (Shenkman, 1988; Spitzer, 2021, p. 220–21). Rifles and pistols still conjure images of fighting for freedom and defending homesteads and families from hostile *others*. Denied or forgotten is the history of gun regulations that expanded along with introduction and proliferation of pistols. Western states had "some of the toughest gun control laws" (Cornell & Kozuskanich, 2013, p. 7, citing Dykstra, 1968).

Gun culture is perpetuated through media—advertising, films, music, and electronic games—as well as through socialization by families and communities. Guns have long been marketed as a great equalizer to empower individuals. Their symbolism as tools to exact justice and promote freedom make them dangerously attractive to young people who may feel wronged and seek vindication or glory. Countering gun culture and imposing restrictions on individual liberties is daunting, even as firearm-related deaths and mass shootings drastically outpace all other developed countries.

Most developed countries can address gun violence with less institutional and social conflict, including Anglosphere democracies. For example, Canada's gun violence problem is less wicked, despite a federal system with provincial governments. Their parliamentary federal government makes governance less protracted; the majority can enact their policies without the veto points characteristic in the U.S. The Canadian Charter of Rights does not include rights of the people to arm themselves, so gun controls are not mired in the same rights-based politics as the U.S. Criminal codes and prosecutions are federal responsibility.

Gun control remains a topic of political campaigns and the gun rights lobby is active, but strong political coalitions and public opinion favors restrictions (Newman & Head, 2017, p. 46–47). Canada and Australia have frontier histories and remote wild places with guns commonly used for hunting and protection, but their gun cultures have not impeded contemporary gun controls. Following mass shootings that shocked and horrified the public, these countries embraced stricter gun controls.

American institutional structures of power also challenge policymaking and channel it. The U.S. Constitution created a federal system with supremacy allotted to national laws and national protections of the peoples' fundamental rights. The First Amendment freedoms of speech, association, press, and petition promote interest group formation and expression, so advocacy pressure on policymakers is built in. In the past 20 years, national policymakers retreated from gun regulation, including letting the assault weapons ban expire and failing to enact universal background checks, so policy innovations devolved to states and localities.

The Second Amendment created constitutional limits to regulating guns at all levels of government, but it does not *preclude* restrictive regulations. The U.S. Supreme Court's Heller decision struck down the D.C. handgun ban reasoning that it "amounts to a prohibition on an entire class of 'arms' that Americans overwhelmingly choose for the lawful purpose of self-defense" (*District of Columbia v. Heller*, 2008, Pt. IV, para. 2).

For the first time, the court interpreted the Second Amendment as guaranteeing an *individual* right to possess firearms unconnected with service in a militia, and found self-defense "a pre-existing right" (*Heller*, 2008, Pt. II, C.). The conservative majority in that case turned away from precedent and amici briefs from historians demonstrated the founders' definitive intent to locate the people's right to bear arms in formal militias and long history of regulating militias, weapons, and ammunition (Cornell & Kozuskanich, 2013, pp. 1–20).

The majority opinion did explicitly state the right to bear arms is "not unlimited" and reaffirmed state interests in regulating firearms for public safety:

> It is not a right to keep and carry any weapon whatsoever in any manner whatsoever and for whatever purpose...The Court's opinion should not be taken to cast doubt on longstanding prohibitions on the possession of firearms by felons and the mentally ill, or laws forbidding the carrying of firearms in sensitive places such as schools and government buildings, or laws imposing conditions and qualifications on the commercial sale of arms. (*Heller*, 2008, Pt. III, para. 1)

Interest groups have long used legal strategies of bringing forth and funding cases to challenge laws; over the last 30 years they have drastically increased the use of amici briefs to shape court interpretations. The NRA and gun rights advocates spent decades promoting legal scholarship and judicial appointments to promote expansive gun rights, enlisting help from friendly politicians and strategically navigating institutional challenges. The Roberts Court and its *Heller* decision reflects the NRA's success, and they continue to seek expansion of self-defense rights beyond the home and into public spaces.

Institutional fragmentation of authority in the U.S. is very high, making it easier to obstruct than to construct policy in the state and national governments. The system of checks and balances between branches creates many veto points. In Congress, most legislation dies in committee and never gets a vote unless it is supported by the majority leadership in both chambers. Powerful lobbies and donors can enlist support and protection for their interests with a small coalition of elected representatives on their side. Divided government, when no party controls both chambers of Congress and the presidency, has stymied federal action on gun policy. Laws, regulations, and executive actions can also be struck down by federal courts when they conflict with the Constitution.

Federal law is superior under the Constitution's supremacy clause, yet federalism allows states to make their own policies where national law or policy has not preempted them. The diverse states have generated very different approaches to gun rights and regulation, reflecting their subnational cultures and structures of power. At all levels of government, active interest groups link the cultural and institutional dimensions of policymaking. Their power can increase conflict and frustrate efforts to overcome fragmented authority. Fragmented authority is even more difficult to overcome when partisan polarization is high and interest groups, such as the NRA, are entrenched on gun policy issues (Haider-Markel & Joslyn, 2001).

Policy experts express concern that gun rights and gun control advocates assert policy prescriptions without adequate evidence of their effectiveness. Research to better understand gun violence and evaluate policy effects offers hope for mitigating this multidimensional problem. Experts assert that complex problems can be made less wicked by reducing uncertainty and promoting evidence-based decisions, but institutional power structures and stakeholder conflict over ideology and polarizing narratives are less easily addressed.

EXPERTS ON GUN VIOLENCE RESEARCH

Gun violence is a public health and criminal justice problem, especially for cities, with significant human and economic costs, direct and indirect. Law enforcement agencies respond to violence that is domestic, workplace, drug-trade, gang-related, and tied to organized crime. Responding to mass shootings and school-based violence is a relatively new challenge. Elected officials and their public safety appointees determine how best to use resources to stem violent crime, historically their top priority.

Mass shootings, including targeted shootings at schools, are rare but beg for appropriate responses: "Some of the most troubling threats currently facing law enforcement are mass casualty events, including attacks within, and violent threats against, our schools" (FBI, 2019). These challenges require federal involvement, information sharing, and coordination with state and local governments. The high social costs and public outcry for action over the last 30 years created the impetus to study gun violence scientifically to inform effective policy in the public interest.

Researchers seek to understand the causes of gun violence in societies and endeavor to explain trends. The CDC declared firearm violence a public health threat in 1983, and institutional studies often take a public health approach. To assist governments and nonprofits in planning programs, the CDC uses a "social-ecological model (SEM) to better understand and prevent violence" that examines societal, community, relationship, and individual risk factors for violence and identifies strategies to reduce risk (CDC, n.d.).

FIREARM HOMICIDES

Gun violence means homicide, rather than suicide or self-defense, to most people and intentional killings are a policy priority. Demographic and environmental factors *positively associated with homicide rates* include population density, percentage of young males, property crime rate, per capita alcohol consumption, and federally licensed firearm dealers per capita (Siegel & Boine, 2019, p. 9). Research examining the "availability of guns" hypothesis to explain gun violence shows, "a change in gun prevalence has a direct effect on weapon choice in robbery and assault, and most importantly, that more guns leads to more gun homicides" (Cook & Goss, 2014, pp. 58–59). These authors point out that "gun use intensifies violence" rather than increasing crime, and root causes of violence rather than guns are more fundamental problems (Cook & Goss, 2014, p. 59).

FIREARM SUICIDES AND FIREARMS IN DOMESTIC VIOLENCE

Guns in the home increase the risk of suicide and deadly domestic violence, which may directly involve or affect children. The U.S. has among the highest rates of suicide by firearm in the world, and over 24K people lost their lives to it in 2018, mostly by firearms.

A robust study of handgun ownership and suicide in California for the period 2004–2016 found, "handgun ownership is associated with a greatly elevated and enduring risk of suicide by firearm" among male and female handgun owners, with men 7.82 times more likely and women 35.15 times more likely to die by suicide (Studdert et al., 2020, p. 2220). Adolescent suicide is a trauma that has long affected families, friends, and school communities. More youth die by suicide every day than by mass shootings each year, and increased access to firearms by youth in the homes or through legal purchases compounds that likelihood.

Uniform Crime reporting for 1997–2016 shows 14% of firearm homicides are committed by an "intimate partner" (Siegel & Boine, 2019, p. 6). Chronic domestic violence is five times more likely to result in death if a gun is in the home (Campbell et al., 2003 as cited by Cook & Goss 2014, p.145). To address this dimension of gun violence, the Violence Against Women Act (1994) banned gun possession and sale to anyone with a restraining order protecting an intimate partner or child, but that information has not been consistently reported to NICS.

MASS SHOOTINGS AND SCHOOL SHOOTINGS

Mass shootings are infrequent compared to gun deaths overall, estimated at "only 1 % of the total firearm-related mortality between 2000 and 2014" (Siegel & Boine, 2019, p. 5). Mass shootings, in terms of number of deaths (from 4–12) or intention, are not defined and counted consistently across agencies and studies. Government sources including the FBI count incidents with lower numbers of persons injured or killed while academic researchers count high-casualty incidents. Scholars also differentiate incidents by intent to better understand mass shootings: "About 20% of mass shootings are classified as mass public shootings, 40% as familicides, and 39% as felony-related mass killings" (Krouse & Richardson, 2015 as cited by RAND, 2020).

The laypersons conception of mass shooting is of the public type that drives gun control initiatives, but that type only counts for a fifth of the incidents. The effects of laws on mass shootings, and the subset of school shootings, are even more challenging to evaluate through quantitative analysis; findings may not be valid and reliable for predicting or preventing future incidents (Kleck, 2009; Koper, 2013; RAND, 2020).

The psychological factors associated with gun violence have gained interest and issue salience in response to unfathomable school shootings and other mass killings at public events. Several adolescent and young adult perpetrators had histories of serious mental illness and made credible threats of violence; some threats were known to schools or reported to law enforcement by family or friends. The National Threat Assessment Center found that attackers in all school shootings "exhibited concerning behaviors" and most communicated their intentions to family and friends (NTAC, 2019, p. 3).

The Parkland shooter was an egregious example of a mentally ill student who was a known threat, and the lack of preventative action was a source of anger for survivors and the community. In response, states have passed red flag laws, which authorize police to temporarily take firearms from people found by a judge to be a danger to themselves or to others. Red flag laws can potentially reduce firearm violence by dangerous persons who passed a background check prior to their illness or before they had a protective order against them (Siegel & Boine, 2019, p. 12).

The Virginia Tech assailant, for example, had prior encounters with the police and mental health professionals but retained his guns. The Sandy Hook Elementary perpetrator was also known to have serious mental illness yet had access to guns in his home. Red flag laws may have prevented them from using firearms to kill so many innocent victims.

Under U.S. federal law (18 U.S.C. Chapter 44), firearms can be seized from someone who is "adjudicated as a mental defective or committed to a mental institution," but that has proven inadequate for stopping mass shooters. The MSD High School shootings spurred more states to pass red flag laws; five states had them before and now 17 states have some version. These new laws show the possibility for bipartisan policy responses after a triggering event and grassroots mobilization.

Red flag laws in the states are being evaluated and will be better understood over the next few years, when impacts and changes in violent outcomes can be tracked. Implementation and unintended impacts will also require attention. Health professionals remind us that mental illness is not uncommon, conditions range from mild to severe, and most people who suffer from mental illness are not dangerous.

Those who suffer mental illness are more likely to be victims than perpetrators of violence. Health professionals warn against dissuading people from seeking medical help, or victim assistance, which would be counterproductive. The American Psychological Association recommendations include a public health approach to gun violence with school-based prevention programs and "enhance(d) access to mental health and substance use services" (APA, 2017).

School shootings are rare but horrific and highly visible. They comprise a very small fraction of overall gun violence, but the trend is alarming. "The number of persons killed and injured by guns in schools varies dramatically from year to year, although it does appear as if both injuries and deaths resulting from school shootings are trending upwards" (Gius, 2018, p. 317).

Another disturbing dimension to school shootings is "significant evidence of contagion in school shootings. An incident is contagious for an average of 13 days and incites an average of at least 0.22 new incidents" (Towers et al., 2015, para. 3). School shootings occur monthly, on average, and are worse in states with more guns per capita. The prevalence of firearm ownership is "significantly associated with the state incidence of mass killings with firearms, and school shootings," but not associated with prevalence of mental illness or strength of firearm legislation (Towers et al., 2015, para. 3). More data and research support is needed to better understand how school shootings are connected to gun proliferation and firearm regulations in the states.

Public health researchers recommend stricter gun controls to stop "preventable" mass shootings, including school shootings, by people who should not have access to guns. Since most guns used by school shooters come from the homes of family or friends, strengthening background checks at the point of sale are inadequate to restrict access.

Dr. Wintemute, a prominent voice in journals and books on preventing gun violence and co-author of the California suicide study, urges policymakers to, "improve background-check policies; require background checks for private-party transfers; require state and local agencies to report prohibiting events; fully implement the existing federal background-check requirement; clarify definitions of prohibiting events; strengthen enforcement efforts; consider a permit-to-purchase approach; prohibit release of firearms until background checks are completed; and enact gun-violence restraining order policies" (2018, p. 1195).

POLICY ANALYSIS AND EVALUATION

Research institutes such as RAND Corporation employ robust methods to synthesize findings from gun violence studies and evaluate the impact of firearm regulations. Multivariate statistical analysis with high levels of confidence can demonstrate the strength of associations between gun control or rights laws and changes in gun violence rates over time. Actionable policy recommendations should be based on best practices in research for validity and reliability.

The variety of studies, research designs, and sources of data are challenging to compare, and debate among experts and uncertainty in evaluating policy outcomes can contribute to policy conflict. Findings from single studies can be misapplied by policymakers and interest groups with ideological biases, partisan pressures, and preconceptions about gun violence.

To aid policymakers, journalists, and the public, RAND and the (Northeast) Regional Gun Violence Research Consortium provide data visualizations and dashboards on gun violence, mass shootings and state laws and legislation. RAND's *Gun Policy Research Review* provides a rigorous assessment of studies and methodologies. Their online Sankey diagram "Gun policies that may decrease outcomes" provides an interactive summary.

The Regional Gun Violence Research Consortium examined the impact of state firearm laws during 1991–2016, looking at laws "most strongly associated with lower rates of firearm homicide" (Siegel & Boine, 2019, p. 4). They studied impacts on homicides (intimate, acquaintance, stranger, & mass), suicides, and unintentional deaths by firearm. Four categories of laws were examined.

One category of laws restrict or regulate *access*—who can purchase or possess firearms, including universal background checks, prohibitions for violent misdemeanor offenders, and restrictive "may issue" or enabling "shall issue" concealed carry permit laws. Another category regulates *types of weapons and ammunition*, including assault weapons bans, large capacity ammunition magazine (LCM) bans, and limits on number of guns that can be purchased. The study also looked at the impact of laws that stipulate *when* firearms may be used, including "stand your ground" laws, and *why* guns are purchased, specifically gun trafficking bans. Their findings are noted below.

WEAPON BANS AND AMMUNITION LIMITS

Banning or restricting types of weapons to reduce gun violence is supported by evidence in Australia and the U.K., as well as some studies of the U.S. A National Institute of Justice–funded analysis of the federal assault weapons ban found "mixed effects" in reducing crimes with these types of weapons, due to its exemptions, grandfathered weapons, ammunition stockpiles, and expiration before the realization of its full effects (Koper, 2013, p. 158).

Yet, crimes with assault weapons clearly declined in six major cities included in the study. The researchers called the limit on large capacity magazines (LCMs) the most important provision of the law, because LCMs are used across weapon types, including semiautomatic handguns, thereby reducing potential firepower and lethality. They concluded a new ban could "help to reduce the number and severity of mass shooting incidents as well as produce a small reduction in shootings overall" (Koper, 2013, p. 168).

RAND's *Gun Policy Research Review* rated as "inconclusive" the evidence that bans on assault weapons and large magazines reduce violent crime or mass shootings. Inconclusive means "inconsistent evidence" across studies or a single study with "uncertain or suggestive effects" (RAND, n.d.). The Regional Gun Violence Consortium (RGVC) report found laws regulating guns and ammunition did not have much of an impact on homicide, but laws that regulate who has access "may have an appreciable impact on firearm homicide" (Siegel & Boine, 2019, p. 9). At this time, it is difficult to see a path to another assault weapon ban in the U.S. given the current political and institutional challenges.

FIREARM ACCESS RESTRICTIONS

People who have a history of violence, or show an imminent threat of violence to themselves or others, pose the greatest risk of committing firearm violence. Opinion polls show supermajorities support limiting access to weapons by dangerous people, and those such restrictions would be more politically feasible to enact than weapon type bans. Access prevention has the potential to reduce school shootings and other gun violence at or near schools.

The 2019 RGVC report included summaries of studies on the effects of state laws and outcomes (Siegel & Boine, 2019, pp. 14–26). Many studies of state background checks or waiting periods find "no significant effect" on homicide rates, but results are inconsistent and gun flows across state borders can undercut these laws. Multiple national studies show "negative association between universal background checks . . . and homicide rates," particularly in urban counties (Siegel & Boine, 2019, p. 7).

The effect on suicides of gun control restrictions (state or county) or absence of restrictions are more striking, though not all studies showed effects. Increased enforcement also reduces death rates. Studies show red flag laws in Connecticut and Indiana significantly reduced suicide rates, and states that lack gun controls are associated with more suicides.

To reduce risks from dangerous people, the researchers suggest policymakers consider laws that:

> 1) Prohibit firearms for those who have committed a "violent misdemeanor or subject to a restraining order, people who have threatened violence, or people with an alcohol-related crime"; 2) "Universal background checks" to prohibit purchases from those groups; and 3) "May issue" laws that give greater

discretion to law enforcement to deny concealed carry permits to high-risk people. (Siegel & Boine, 2019, p. 12)

Protecting children from gun violence is a policy priority in several states and laws that reduce youth access to guns have made a difference in reducing deaths. A recent study published by the National Academies of Science found that child access prevention laws demonstrated a strong association with lower firearms deaths (Schell et al., 2020). The study also examined the effects of gun rights laws, specifically right-to-carry and stand your ground laws for the period 1970 to 2016.

The authors found "state laws restricting firearm storage and use are associated with a subsequent 11% decrease in the firearms-related death rate" when the state had no right to carry or stand your ground laws (p. 1). RAND's 2020 updates to *The Science of Gun Policy* report highlight the findings that child-access prevention and safe storage laws "reduce self-inflicted fatal and nonfatal firearm injuries . . . among youth," and stand your ground laws are "associated with increases in firearm homicides" (Smart et al., 2020, p. 2). They also report "moderate evidence that waiting periods reduce firearm suicides and total homicides" (p. 2). These gun access restrictions protect child welfare directly and indirectly, and RAND recommends states consider adopting these types of laws.

GUN REGULATION AND EFFECTS ON SCHOOL SHOOTINGS

School shooting incidents lead to calls for gun control legislation and several states have passed or strengthened gun laws in response. Policy economist Mark Gius (2018) analyzed the effects of federal and state assault weapons bans, federal and state background checks, and concealed carry laws on school shootings. His regression analysis found that assault weapon bans resulted in significantly fewer casualties from school shootings, including a 54% reduction in the number of victims. The other gun laws did not show a statistically significant effect on victimization.

States' economic and social factors, used as control variables, showed "much greater effects on the number of shooting victims than did the assault weapons ban" (p. 320). States with above-average unemployment and gun ownership rates, greater than average alcohol consumption, and larger student-age populations suffer greater firearm casualties. The author concludes that it is "unclear if gun control is the most appropriate policy to use to reduce the number school shooting victims" (p. 320).

RAND rates as "uncertain" the evidence from four studies of the assault weapons ban, including Gius's, because of methodological concerns and question whether effects come from "change in the federal law versus from changes in state policy" (RAND, 2020). The complexity of designing and conducting quantitative studies is enormous and communication of their findings can overwhelm policymakers trying to rely on evidence-based studies.

SCHOOL SECURITY MEASURES

Gun violence on or near school grounds includes homicides, assaults, suicides, and unintentional discharges, as well as more rare targeted mass shootings (Everytown for Gun Safety, 2020). School-based policies can also benefit from evidence-based decisions. Schools have responded by hiring private security or school resource officers (SROs), usually armed, to deter and respond to incidents of violence.

Access controls are also typical. Most schools have not embraced metal detectors because of cost; approximately 10% of schools have daily screenings (Addington, 2009). The desirability of these responses is debated from many perspectives, and evaluations of their efficacy are often based on the subjective perceptions of school administrators.

Studies examining the benefits of SROs show "mixed results," and there is little evidence that SROs reduce violence in schools (Jonson, 2017, p. 962). Armed SROs and police on campus didn't deter the shooters at Columbine or Virginia Tech. Electronic access controls are insufficient if perpetrators are students or staff with ID access. Metal detectors can deter students bringing in weapons and some schools have reported benefits (Hankin et al., 2011). Both types of control can be evaded when perpetrators shoot their way in, as happened at Sandy Hook Elementary and Red Lake Senior High School in Minnesota.

Schools have moved beyond traditional lockdown and now include multi-option response programs with "three core concepts: (a) leaving the scene of the shooting, (b) locking down and barricading, and (c) actively resisting the shooter" (Jonson, 2017, p. 966). These are listed in order of desirability and context determines the appropriate response, but research is inadequate to demonstrate their efficacy. The Virginia Tech case provided a natural experiment to compare responses, and barricading and fleeing were associated with fewer fatalities, so "when individuals take a more active multi-option response approach to shootings, they appear to have a higher likelihood of surviving such an incident" (p. 968).

Efforts to identify potential shooters and evaluate their risk of violence are also fraught with uncertainty about effects and unintended consequences. The

National Threat Assessment Center found "no profile of student attacker" or type of school and multiple motives, although "grievances with other classmates" was most common in their study of 41 incidents occurring 2008–2017 (NTAC, 2019, p. 3). A desire for vengeance and the second most common motive, a "desire to kill," (NTAC, 2019, p. 15) suggests a disturbing cultural problem connected to gun mythology and media.

The threat assessment approach promoted by the U.S. Secret Service and Department of Homeland Security is controversial, associated with national security missions and preventing terrorism not learning environments that depend on trust. "Profiling, guided professional judgment, automated decision-making" can be inappropriate or harmful while failing to prevent planned school-based attacks (Reddy et al., 2001, p.157). Advocates also promote school-based interventions, including counseling and student support programs that may prevent gun violence among youth and reduce negative impacts on students and staff.

PROSPECTS FOR POLICY ACTION ON GUN VIOLENCE

School communities are tackling the problems of gun violence with campus-based efforts and through democratic mobilization for gun control policies. But gun violence as a policy problem is uniquely wicked in the U.S., particularly at the federal level due to political, cultural, institutional, and legal factors that inhibit adoption and implementation of restrictions on gun rights. Bipartisan commitment to improve existing firearm access limits is not impossible and shows promise for mitigating gun violence based on research.

Political mobilization in the face of an increasing number of mass shootings and strong public support for strengthening background checks could push the national government to act, but it would likely require presidential leadership and unified government. Incremental changes, such as increased funding for gun violence research and better reporting procedures to strengthen the national background check system are proceeding, despite partisan divides.

State-level policymaking is more responsive to popular demands, but some states adopted laws to strengthen gun rights that have increased firearm deaths. State laws that restrict access to guns by dangerous people have been shown to reduce homicides and suicides and may reduce mass shooting fatalities, including those at schools. Policy improvements in laws and their implementation offer hope, and successful policies may diffuse across states.

Newer state laws limiting types of weapons and LCMs show potential for reducing lethality but still lack conclusive evidence of effectiveness in reducing firearm deaths. These regulations continue to be tested in federal courts by gun rights advocates, and recent conflicting decisions in the circuit courts about ammunition limits will require clarification from the U.S. Supreme Court. Legal outcomes are uncertain in the current period of judicial activism regarding the Second Amendment. If gun rights activists roll back restrictions, we should expect increases in gun violence, such as acquisition of guns by young people who may harm themselves or others at or near schools.

Causes of gun violence at schools, including mass shootings, are still not well understood and the efficacy of firearm access prevention laws and school safety measures need further evaluation. Applying scientific methods to formulate policies can improve outcomes, if the politics of gun debates doesn't marginalize scientific voices. To overcome policy gridlock, national and state governments might seek "new gun laws but not those that violate core rights" (Bennett, 2008, p. 492).

Constitutional law and American public opinion have supported both gun rights and reasonable restrictions. Shifting away from language of control that connotes violating the gun rights of law-abiding gun owners, focusing instead on dangerous persons, may be part of the answer. Devising firearm regulations supported by evidence and tailored to specific problem dimensions, such as limiting youth access, could offer a healthier path forward for schools and their communities.

REFERENCES

Addington, L. A. (2009). Cops and cameras: Public school security as a policy response to Columbine. *American Behavioral Scientist, 52*(10), 1426–1446.

American Psychological Association. (2017, May). *Gun violence*. https://www.apa.org/advocacy/gun-violence/

Bennett, M. (2008). Misfire: How the debate over gun rights ignores reality. *Albany Government Law Review, 1*(2), 482–495.

Centers for Disease Control. (n.d.). The social-ecological model: A framework for violence prevention. https://www.cdc.gov/violenceprevention/pdf/sem_framewrk-a.pdf

Cook, P. J. & Goss, K. A. (2014). *The gun debate: What everyone needs to know*. Oxford University Press.

Cornell & Kozuskanich. (2013). *The Second Amendment on trial: Critical essays on District of Columbia v. Heller*. University of Massachusetts Press.

District of Columbia, et al., v. Heller, 554 US 570 (2008).

Edwards, G. C. III, Barrett, A., & Peake, J. (1997). The legislative impact of divided government. *American Journal of Political Science, 41*(2), 545–563.

Everytown For Gun Safety. (2020, May 19). *Keeping our schools safe: A plan for preventing mass shootings and ending all gun violence in American schools*. https://everytownresearch.org/report/a-plan-for-preventing-mass-shootings-and-ending-all-gun-violence-in-american-schools/

Federal Bureau of Investigation. (2019, March 13). Gun violence prevention and enforcement: Statement before the House Appropriations Committee, Subcommittee on Commerce, Justice, Science, and Related Agencies. https://www.fbi.gov/news/testimony/gun-violence-prevention-and-enforcement

Giffords Law Center to Prevent Gun Violence. (2020). Annual gun law scorecard. https://lawcenter.giffords.org/scorecard/

Gius, M. (2018). The effects of state and federal gun control laws on school shootings. *Applied Economics Letters 25*(5), 317–320.

Goss, K. A. (2006). *Disarmed: The Missing Movement for Gun Control in America.* Princeton University Press.

Goss, K. A. (2012, December) America's missing popular movement for gun control. Scholars Strategy Network. https://scholars.org/sites/scholars/files/ssn_basic_facts_goss_on_gun_control.pdf

Gramlich, J. (2019, October 16). What the data says about gun deaths in the U.S. Pew Research Center. https://www.pewresearch.org/fact-tank/2019/08/16/what-the-data-says-about-gun-deaths-in-the-u-s/

Gramlich, J. & Schaeffer, K. (2019, October 22). Seven facts about guns in the U.S. Pew Research Center. https://www.pewresearch.org/fact-tank/2019/10/22/facts-about-guns-in-united-states/

Grinshteyn, E. & Hemenway, D. (2016). Violent death rates: The US compared with other high-income OECD countries, 2010. *American Journal of Medicine, 129*(3), 266–73. https://pubmed.ncbi.nlm.nih.gov/26551975/

Haider-Markel, D. P. & Joslyn, M. R. (2001). Gun policy, opinion, tragedy, and blame attribution: The conditional influence of issue frames. *Journal of Politics, 63*(2), 520–543.

Hankin, A., Hertz, M., & Simon, T. (2011). Impacts of metal detector use in schools: Insights from 15 years of research. *Journal of School Health, 81*(2), 100–106. https://doi.org/10.1111/j.1746-1561.2010.00566.x

Harvard University. (2018, April). Institute of Politics spring 2018 youth poll. https://iop.harvard.edu/spring-2018-poll

Hofstadter, R. (1970, October). America as a gun culture. *American Heritage, 21*(6).

Jonson, C. L. (2017). Preventing school shootings: The effectiveness of safety measures. *Victims & Offenders 12*(6), 956–973. https://doi.org/10.1080/15564886.2017.1307293

Karp, A. (2018, June). Estimating global civilian-held firearms numbers. *Small Arms Survey.* Graduate Institute of Geneva. http://www.smallarmssurvey.org/fileadmin/docs/T-Briefing-Papers/SAS-BP-Civilian-Firearms-Numbers.pdf

Kennett, L. & Anderson, J. L. (1975). *The gun in America: The origins of a national dilemma.* Greenwood Press.

Kleck, G. (2009). Mass shootings in schools: The worst possible case for gun control. *American Behavioral Scientist, 52*(10), 1447–1464.

Koper, C. S. (2013). America's experience with the federal assault weapons ban, 1994-2004. In D. W. Webster & J. S. Vernick (Eds.), *Reducing gun violence in America* (pp. 157–171). Johns Hopkins University Press.

Lepore, J. (2012, April 23). Battleground America. *New Yorker*. https://www.newyorker.com/magazine/2012/04/23/battleground-america#

Lott, J. R., Jr. (1998). *More Guns, Less Crime*. University of Chicago Press.

Merry, M. K. (2016). Constructing policy narratives in 140 characters or less: The case of gun policy organizations. *Policy Studies Journal, 44*(4), 373–395.

Murray, P. (2013). The secret of scale. *Stanford Social Innovation Review 11*(4), 32–39. https://ssir.org/articles/entry/the_secret_of_scale#

National Threat Assessment Center (U.S.). (2019). Protecting America's schools: A U.S. Secret Service analysis of targeted school violence. U.S. Department of Homeland Security, U.S. Secret Service, National Threat Assessment Center. https://permanent.fdlp.gov/gpo128400/usss-analysis-of-targeted-school-violence.pdf

Newman, J., & Head, B. (2017). The national context of wicked problems: Comparing policies on gun violence in the U.S., Canada, and Australia. *Journal of Comparative Policy Analysis: Research and Practice, 19*(1), 40–53, https://doi.org/10.1080/13876988.2015.1029334

Parsons, C., Thompson, M., Weigend Vargas, E., & Rocco, G. (2018, May 4). America's youth under fire: The devastating impact of gun violence on young people. Center for American Progress. https://www.americanprogress.org/issues/guns-crime/reports/2018/05/04/450343/americas-youth-fire/

RAND Corporation (2020, April 22). Effects of assault weapon and high-capacity magazine bans on mass shootings. Gun Policy in America. https://www.rand.org/research/gun-policy/analysis/mass-shootings.html

RAND Corporation (n.d.). Gun Policy Research Review. Gun Policy in America. https://www.rand.org/research/gun-policy/analysis.html

Reddy, M., Borum, R., Berglund, J., Vossekuil, B., Fein, R., & Modzeleski, W. (2001). Evaluating risk for targeted violence in schools: Comparing risk assessment, threat assessment, and other approaches. *Psychology in the Schools, 38*(2), 157–172. https://doi.org/10.1002/pits.1007

Schaeffer, K. (2019, October 16). Share of Americans who favor stricter gun laws has increased since 2017. Pew Research Center. https://www.pewresearch.org/fact-tank/2019/10/16/share-of-americans-who-favor-stricter-gun-laws-has-increased-since-2017/

Schell, T. L., Cefalu, M., Griffin, B. A., Smart, R., and Morral, A. R. (2020, June 15). Changes in firearm mortality following the implementation of state laws regulating firearm access and use. *PNAS: Proceedings* of the National Academies of Science. https://doi.org/10.1073/pnas.1921965117

Schmidt, M. S. (2015, July 10). Background check flaw let Dylann Roof buy gun, F.B.I. says. *New York Times*. https://www.nytimes.com/2015/07/11/us/background-check-flaw-let-dylann-roof-buy-gun-fbi-says.html

Shenkman, R. (1988). *Legends, lies, and cherished myths of American history*. Morrow.

Siegel, M., & Boine, C. (2019, March 29). *What are the most effective policies in reducing gun homicides?* Policy brief. Rockefeller Institute of Government.

Slotkin, R. (1985). *The fatal environment: The myth of the frontier in the age of industrialization 1800-1890*. Atheneum.

Smart, R., Morral, A. R., Smucker, S., Cherney, S., Schell, T. L., Peterson, S., Ahluwalia, S. C., Cefalu, M., Xenakis, L., Ramchand, R., & Gresenz, C. R. (2020). *The Science of gun policy: A critical synthesis of research evidence on the effects of gun policies in the United States* (2nd ed.). RAND Corporation. https://www.rand.org/pubs/research_reports/RR2088-1.html

Spitzer, R. J. (2021). *The politics of gun control* (8th ed.). Routledge.

Studdert, D., Zhang, Y., Swanson, S., Rodden, J., Holsinger, E., Spittal, M., Wintemute, G., & Miller, M. (2020, June). Handgun ownership and suicide in California. *New England Journal of Medicine, 382*(23), 2220–9. https://www.nejm.org/doi/10.1056/NEJMsa1916744

Tarrow, S. (1998). *Power in movement: Social movements and contentious politics* (2nd ed.). Cambridge University Press.

Towers, S., Gomez-Lievano, A., Khan, M., Mubayi, A., & Castillo-Chavez, C. (2015). Contagion in mass killings and school shootings. *PLoS ONE, 10*(7): e0117259. https://doi.org/10.1371/journal.pone.0117259

Warnick, B., Johnson, B. A., & Rocha, S. (2018, February 14). Why security measures won't stop school shootings. *The Conversation.* https://theconversation.com/why-security-measures-wont-stop-school-shootings-90738

Wintemute, G. J. (2018). How to stop mass shootings. *New England Journal of Medicine, 379*(13): 1193–1196.

Chapter 2

Considering Ostracism Events as a Precursor to School Shootings

Fatima Albrehi and Lukas Pelliccio

> "A student in a neighboring town compiled a very detailed plan of how he was going to go about shooting up his school. He created a list of the students and faculty he was going to go after. The time period between the threat being reported and when he was taken into custody was a very real and scary time for my school district. We were all on edge because we didn't know where the potential shooter was."—Kassandra, graduate student & new teacher

Over the past three decades, the news media, public, politicians, administrators, law enforcement, and parents alike have all tried to make sense of the school shootings that have plagued the United States. Many want to understand what factors could possibly drive someone to commit such heinous acts and what can be done to stop them from happening again. In the past, bad parenting, access to guns, popular music, and mental health have all been used to explain the actions of school shooters.

Often, the media and the public immediately investigate whether the perpetrator was bullied. Bullying is a well-studied phenomenon and is defined by researchers as intentionally hurtful messages that are repeated and used to create or reinforce a power imbalance between communicators (Volk et al., 2014). Bullying is used too often as a simplistic, catch-all term that embodies any negative communication that young people experience. By relying on reductive answers, administrators, media, parents, and the public fail to acknowledge the many more covert and subtle forms of communication that take place in young peoples' social lives that can have potentially serious effects on school shooters' worldviews and self-esteem.

Ostracism is one particular type of communication that is detrimental for teens' emotional well-being that differs from bullying. Researchers define ostracism as the exclusion of an individual or group by another individual or group. Kipling Williams, a scholar most known for his research on ostracism as a phenomenon, asserts that ostracism consists of interactions where people are denied access to social resources through ignoring, silencing, and banishment (2002).

Ostracism differs from bullying in that it can be unintentional or indirectly communicated. People can be ostracized from groups by not being invited to gatherings, not being spoken to, or not being acknowledged in social settings. In modern social environments, ostracism can be communicated on social media, group chats, as well as in face-to-face interactions. Research shows that being ostracized can initiate very serious negative psychological effects for a target that are unique and can ultimately lead to antisocial behaviors, such as lashing out at others (Williams et al., 2005).

It is important to consider the frequency and severity of ostracism as we explore the prior lived experiences of school shooters to better understand how such messages impacted their decision making. There are certainly many different factors that influence a school shooter's actions. It is not to say that bullying, access to guns or bad parenting are not important to consider, but rather that ostracism is a unique communication experience with serious negative effects on human beings, and therefore requires more attention.

A deeper look at the previous communication interactions of the perpetrators of school shootings often reveals the stories of individuals who were not included in groups, were broadly ostracized by their peers, or were rejected by a desired relational partner. Whether it was a friend, lover, or teammate, some school shooters experienced several serious rejection messages that appeared to be connected to their mental state and lead inexorably to their abhorrent acts (Betts & Hinsz, 2013; Leary et al., 2003). For some, the cumulative effect of minor and major messages of ostracism resulted in deep hurt that was much more significant than overt bullying.

Researchers, journalists, parents, administrators, and society at large should begin to give more attention to the importance of school shooters being ostracized, ignored, and rejected, to gain a deeper and more nuanced understanding of the everyday communication that contributes to these perpetrators' worldviews. We acknowledge that conversations surrounding access to firearms, mental health, and other causes are necessary, but subtle and overt moments of chronic ostracism and rejection can cumulatively create long-lasting and damaging effects on adolescents.

The school shootings that took place at Santa Fe High School, Marjory Douglas Stoneman High School, and Marysville-Pilchuck High School reveal forms of ostracism and rejection communication that took place leading up to the shootings. These three shootings resulted in many casualties and received significant media coverage, which ensures that there is ample detail on these events. These reports generated evidence of communicative moments of ostracism and interpersonal rejection that influenced the shooter.

In our analysis we differentiate ostracism from bullying based on Williams's (2002) conceptualization of the phenomenon, ground it in a communication-based approach, and make suggestions for how school administrators, news media, and other stakeholders can refocus their attention to implement ostracism support strategies.

EXPERIENCING SOCIAL DEATH DUE TO MESSAGES OF OSTRACISM

Leading researchers characterize ostracism as the experience of being ignored or excluded by others (Williams, 2002). Communication such as giving someone the cold shoulder, verbally telling someone they are not welcomed, ignoring someone in a conversation, forgetting to invite someone to a party, or not being included in an expected in-group are all considered forms of ostracism (Williams & Zadro, 2005; Pelliccio, 2018). The key to understanding ostracism, though, is that it can be communicated intentionally or unintentionally, with plausible deniability.

The ostracizer may simply have forgotten to verbally include a target because they are preoccupied with other goals or do not have as much of a relationship with a particular member of a group. Although this is unintentional communication, it can still create the same negative psychological state for a target. As long as an individual feels like they are not being included or are being ignored, they are referred to as a "target" because they are the object of the ostracism message. From this, a target endures a type of "social death," thereby ceasing to have a meaningful existence in groups they were, or desire to be, a part of.

Researchers suggest that even the most subtle communication, such as averted eye contact (Williams & Nida, 2017), uncomfortable silence (Rittenour et al., 2019), or receiving no "likes" on Facebook (Reich et al., 2018), can trigger an individual's sense of being ostracized and cause hurt, depending on the context and the interpretation by the target (Pelliccio, 2018).

Ostracism scholars further suggest that when an individual perceives a message of ostracism as a threat, they will experience threats to four specific psychological needs including: belonging, self-esteem, control, and meaningful existence (Eck et al., 2017; Gonsalkorale & Williams, 2007; Van Zalk & Smith, 2019). The need for belonging is the desire to be connected and involved with others and the recognition that we are valued members of a particular group. Self-esteem is how we feel about ourselves. Control is our sense of autonomy and ability to influence our environment. Meaningful existence is the need to feel as though our existence matters to others (Williams et al., 2005).

If one fundamental need becomes threatened, the others may be threatened as well because they are intertwined. As a result, when someone is ostracized, they may turn on themselves and begin thinking very negatively (Williams & Nida, 2017). They may question whether they are good enough for others and whether they will ever be accepted by anyone again.

After receiving a message of ostracism, the psychological experience can be divided into three stages: reflexive, reflective, and resignation (Williams, 2009). These three stages influence how targets communicate with others.

First, the reflexive stage happens immediately after a message of ostracism is interpreted and the target feels a myriad of negative emotions such as shock, pain, confusion, guilt, inferiority, anger, and/or sadness. Studies show that targets experience physical changes as well, such as sweaty palms, increased heart rate, and/or increased blood pressure (Kelly et al., 2012). Researchers further argue that our reaction to ostracism communication is part of a natural alert system in human beings that signals to us that we are being excluded from something important and that this exclusion may be detrimental to our survival (Buss, 1990; Gonsalkorale & Williams, 2007; Kerr & Levine, 2008).

Second, in the reflective stage, targets of ostracism turn their attention inward and attempt to cope with the pain of being ostracized (Williams & Gerber, 2005). Here, the target tries to make attributions as to why they were ostracized. For some, they cast the blame on others by suggesting that their negative feelings are the fault of the other person or people. Others turn on themselves and begin blaming themselves for their exclusion. They may also use communication to reach out to others in an effort to reduce their uncertainty and make sense of the messages they received (Pelliccio, 2018).

After experiencing ostracism from one desired group, they may exhibit prosocial behaviors such as increased friendliness and helpfulness to others to foster inclusion in a new group (Williams et al., 2005). Conversely, they may exhibit antisocial behaviors where they become more aggressive, demeaning, or hurtful towards others as they retaliate for being ostracized (Baumeister et al., 2007). Whether prosocial or antisocial, research shows that ostracism fosters socially susceptible people who are unstable and more likely to be influenced by others' communication (Carter-Sowell et al., 2008).

Finally, in the resignation stage, targets of ostracism accept their status as outcasts and reduce efforts to communicate with a desired group (Buelow et al., 2015; Williams, 2002). In this stage, it becomes clear to the target that their attempts at obtaining recognition and/or acceptance—whether through pro- or antisocial behaviors/communication—are useless (Riva et al., 2017).

At its most severe, the target of chronic ostracism may engage in extreme antisocial behaviors like self-harm or suicide in an attempt to regain a sense of control (Chen et al., 2020). One extreme action may be carrying out a shooting. Some studies conclude that ostracism was a contributing factor to many of the school shootings that took place in the United States over the past few decades (Leary et al., 2003).

OSTRACISM COMMUNICATION AND SCHOOL SHOOTINGS

Although ostracism conceptually overlaps with constructs like bullying, in that someone can intentionally ostracize another as a means of bullying them, more often ostracism is communicated in subtle, covert, and nuanced ways that may or may not be intentional or visible to others (Pelliccio & Nickell, 2018). Rather than telling someone face-to-face that they are not wanted, communicators may simply ignore a target and therefore deny their social and/or physical existence. Though the target is not being repeatedly and overtly bullied, they certainly experience emotional pain as a result.

The distinction between ostracism and bullying is important as we look deeper into the cases of three school shooters who carefully crafted plans to murder their peers. Although they may have experienced episodes of bullying, romantic rejections and chronic ostracism were communicated to them frequently and had a significant impact on their mental states. For example, Leary and colleagues (2003) conducted a case study of 15 different school shootings and found that ostracism alone was not a causal factor, but that it could be if combined with other existing conditions such as mental health and/or obsession with firearms. Thus, it may not be that a single ostracism experience leads to school shootings, but that it can be an important factor to consider amongst others.

Furthermore, it is important to understand that the communication of ostracism is a cumulative experience for an individual. Researchers argue that all communication exists in a "chain of utterances" and that no message is communicated in a bubble (Baxter & Norwood, 2015). Our interpretation of communication is highly influenced by messages that come before, during, and after any given message. Therefore, meanings change over time, and when we receive a message, our interpretation is affected by other messages in the chain of utterances.

In terms of ostracism communication, this notion suggests that all the "minor" moments of cold shoulder, not being invited to gatherings, being silenced or receiving the silent treatment, and/or romantic rejection, can actually add up overtime to create a dangerous cumulative effect (Pelliccio, 2018). Such experiences may be considered "minor" in the moment, but experienced repeatedly over time, have a significant effect on one's fundamental psychological well-being. Receiving ongoing messages of ostracism add up to a collection of interactions that carry meaning. Thus, communication researchers suggest that as we begin to analyze school shooters' interactions prior to the shooting, we should acknowledge the minor moments alongside the more significant ones to fully understand how communication overtime can affect individuals.

OSTRACISM, ROMANTIC REJECTION, AND SCHOOL SHOOTINGS

Studies suggest that romantic rejection is a specific type of ostracism communication that can have a significant impact on some potential school shooters. In a study of 126 school shootings in thirteen different countries, researchers found that about 30% of perpetrators experienced some type of romantic rejection before carrying out the shooting (Sommer et al., 2014). It is difficult for researchers to discern why romantic rejections influence some individuals so profoundly.

Farr (2019) asserts that such experiences are emasculating for young males, and that by killing people publicly, the shooter reverses the injury to his self-esteem with the ultimate display of violent masculinity. Farr (2018) further argues that the communication of romantic rejection negatively affects the credibility of shooters and their social status. Instead of communicating their sadness and sense of powerlessness over being rejected in socially acceptable ways, these adolescent boys let their emotions build up to the point where they view violently lashing out as a masculine way to reframe their "feminine" emotions.

Before we begin to examine the communication of ostracism in the social interactions in our case studies of Dimitrios Pagourtzis, Nikolas Cruz, and Jaylen Fryberg, it is important to note that no individual or group of people is responsible for these horrific acts of violence other than the school shooters themselves. We have no intention to place blame on anyone who ostracized or romantically rejected a school shooter before they became violent. No one should expect to be a victim simply because they turned someone down, nor should they feel obligated to include everyone in everything they do.

Communicating ostracism takes place all the time in our everyday lives. Our intention here is to recognize the unintended pain caused by ostracism experiences for some already fragile individuals, so that we can offer them better social support and begin taking peers' concerns more seriously. Whether for the protection of adolescent females, or social support for rejected young people who do not have the tools to cope with the pain of being excluded, we will demonstrate that episodes of ostracism require more attention so that we can create safer environments for all stakeholders.

Santa Fe High School Shooting

On May 18, 2018, Dimitrios Pagourtzis entered Santa Fe High School by damaging a door window in an art classroom. As he sang, "Another One Bites the Dust," he callously murdered ten of his peers and injured 14. It was a tragedy that shook the nation and received much attention in the media.

After Pagourtzis was arrested, many interviews were conducted with individuals who interacted with him before the shooting happened. Some of the interviewees recounted moments of overt, intentional bullying that Pagourtzis was subjected to. Published testimonies suggested that Pagourtzis was picked on by his football coaches at the school for "smelling bad" (BBC, 2018a). Pagourtzis's father also claimed that his son's history of being bullied was the primary catalyst for the shooting. School administrators denied these claims.

Other testimonies revealed that Pagourtzis was socially and romantically ostracized by his peers in both subtle and overt ways and that these moments were significant to his mental state. Pagourtzis is often described as the "odd one out" who *chose* not to engage in typical social behaviors such as conversing with peers. However, people can still communicate exclusion without being conscious of being the source of ostracism (Williams, 2002); an ostracism source's lack of consciousness regarding their position further highlights how subtle ostracism can be.

Classmates' testimonies go beyond the father's assertion that he was bullied and expose the nuances of communication. For example, Pagourtzis was described as someone who mostly kept to himself, as a "weird loner" who "never seemed right" and "wore a trench coat almost every day" which could have been his way of conveying affinity with the Columbine shooters (Perez et al., 2018). In an interview with the *New York Times*, a teacher at Santa Fe High stated that Pagourtzis was "quiet, but he wasn't quiet in a creepy way" (Fernandez et al., 2018). Others claimed that, "Every time you'd try to start a conversation with him, he'd just kind of like laugh, and wouldn't really continue with the conversation. . . . He didn't like interacting with other students."

A friend explained that Pagourtzis's father was a "control freak" and that Dimitrios was not allowed to go anywhere when his father would visit Greece for several months (Bethea, 2018). This effectively excluded him from social events and disconnected him from others for long periods of time and further shows that ostracism can be communicated unintentionally but still negatively impact a target.

However, one of the most substantial ostracism events occurred when Pagourtzis suffered a crushing romantic rejection. According to reports, Pagourtzis was particularly interested in a female classmate, who he pursued for several months prior to the shooting (Perez et al., 2018). This classmate continuously rejected Pagourtzis advances. The girl's mother stated in an interview that one day her daughter stood up to Pagourtzis in class, in front of their peers, and verbally proclaimed that she would never go out with him. Pagourtzis was publicly humiliated by this rejection message.

A week later, Pagourtzis carried out the premeditated murder of his classmates; one of his victims was the girl who had rejected him. The girl was an innocent victim who rejected his advances but Pagourtzis likely had no ability to cope with the aftermath of receiving such a message of ostracism. This incident indicates that Pagourtzis was still processing emotions of anger and feelings of inferiority in the reflexive and reflective stages of ostracism (Williams, 2002).

Many news articles focused either on how Pagourtzis was an honor roll student and a football player who was plagued by mental health issues, or the tortured victim of bullying (Perez et al., 2018). Yet, if we examine the events that led up to the shooting itself, they confirm our supposition that the cumulative experiences of ostracism were an important antecedent to Pagourtzis's actions. Ostracism research suggests that when Pagourtzis was rejected romantically, it resulted in a negative psychological reaction in which he experienced a harsh initial shock, followed by cognitive threats to his sense of belonging, control, self-esteem, and meaningful existence.

The public nature of the episode would make the experience even more hurtful because the insult was magnified by the silent witness of bystanders. By publicly targeting his failed love interest in the shooting, Pagourtzis's action communicated his intention to restore both a sense of control over events and his wounded masculinity.

Social and romantic relationships are often a priority for American adolescents and facing rejection can leave a young person in an adverse state, especially if it is made public. Without a support system or the tools to cope, targets of ostracism may ruminate in feelings of anger, pain, betrayal, and inferiority without communicating their need for support.

In Pagourtzis's case, he attempted to make sense of feelings of loss and humiliation experienced in the reflexive stage of ostracism. In the reflective stage, he attempted to cope, but due to the cumulative weight of various ostracism events, he ruminated in the resignation stage and blamed his suffering on the girl who rejected him, which served as the tipping point of accumulated ostracism events. The shooting was a solution to his troubles by way of reasserting control publicly and salving his self-perception of inferiority and exclusion.

Classmates' descriptions of Pagourtzis as a "loner" who "kept to himself" and who "never seemed right" highlights his chronic ostracism and outgroup status. Despite Pagourtzis being on the roster of his school's "beloved" football team, he was not granted insider social status among his peers or accepted as such by the adults affiliated with the team. His teammates explained that he mostly kept to himself and eventually quit the team when he was moved from JV to Varsity (BBC, 2018a).

Few reports go into any detail about the many minor and subtle ostracism experiences that Pagourtzis may have experienced in the locker room or on the field, but his initial plan to commit suicide suggests that he was chronically ostracized. It is clear that Pagourtzis believed that he did not matter or belong in the social circles of his peers and therefore experienced a kind of social death.

At the time of the shooting, the public and media fixated on Pagourtzis's mental health, the music he listened to, gun control, and brief reports of bullying. However, we believe that administrators, news reporters, law enforcement, researchers, and the public need to give more attention to the seemingly minor ostracism experiences to understand how they cumulatively affect Pagourtzis and other school shooters. It may not have been the primary motivator, but it certainly contributed in some degree.

Marjory Stoneman Douglas High School Shooting

While reports about Dimitrios Pagourtzis largely framed him as a good student who showed no signs of danger to others, Nikolas Cruz of Marjory Stoneman Douglas High School had a history of antisocial and aggressive behaviors that were known to administrators and law enforcement alike. On February 18, 2018, Cruz took an Uber to his high school in Parkland, Florida, and proceeded to go on a shooting rampage that lasted six minutes. In that brief span of time, Cruz killed 17 people and injured another 17. The shooting garnered international attention and spawned the student-led movement widely known as "Never Again: March for Our Lives," which demanded a broad overhaul of legislation related to gun rights in the United States.

The conversation stemming from Cruz's actions mainly focused on how his rampage could have been prevented given that there were so many red flags. Nikolas Cruz had a history of being in trouble. School administrators received tips that Cruz was a school shooting threat in 2016 and 2017. The FBI learned about a YouTube user called "nikolas cruz" who communicated intent to attack school mates but could not trace the account directly to Cruz

(Sacks, 2018). The FBI tip line also received a notice in January of 2018 that Cruz had made a death threat against someone (Benner et al., 2018).

As one of Cruz's peers stated after the terrible event, "Everyone had in their minds if anybody was going to do it, it was going to be him" (Darrah & Gaydos, 2018). As the media converged on Parkland, they largely focused on Cruz's mental health and access to firearms. Interviews at the time suggested that he was "stressed out all the time." They pointed to the fact that Cruz was admitted to a mental health facility several years before the shooting and at one point was diagnosed as having autism spectrum disorder (Burch et al., 2018).

In addition, it is evident that Cruz was also physically, socially, and romantically ostracized throughout his life in both overt and subtle ways. Cruz grew up as an orphan and had a tumultuous childhood where individuals who might have offered stability and support, regularly entered and then exited his life. He was adopted at a very young age after his parents passed away. In middle school, he transferred between schools six times in three years (Craig et al., 2018). In 2014 he was sent to a school for children with emotional and learning disabilities for a period of time and was eventually expelled from Marjory Stoneman Douglas High School in 2017 for disciplinary infractions. A former classmate revealed that "he got kicked out of two private schools" and "was held back twice" (McLaughlin & Park, 2018).

Around the same time that he was expelled from high school, his adopted parents passed away. In the period leading up to the shooting, he was constantly being moved from house to house, and did not have a long-term home or family. For much of his life, the outside world communicated to him in a variety of forms that his presence was unwanted.

While the U.S. press focused on Cruz's mental health, the BBC (2018b), described Cruz as a depressed loner in high school, who was socially isolated from his peers and "an outcast" who did not have "many friends." They quoted peers referring to him as "creepy." Whether it was at home or school, he was constantly on the fringes of acceptance, never truly included.

One individual who ignored Cruz appeared to have had a significant impact on him. According to a math teacher at the school, Cruz was obsessed with a girl in his class. Cruz's interactions with the girl became so unnerving that the teacher became worried that Cruz was actually stalking the girl, who constantly rejected his advances. The classmate reported Cruz multiple times to school officials between 2016 and 2017. She also reported that Cruz was physically abusive towards a classmate he briefly dated and threatened her family (ABC News, 2018). An investigator's report from the Florida Department of Children and Families noted that prior to the shooting, Cruz had exhibited "behavior changes" following a recent breakup. Cruz was also reported to have expressed a desire to purchase a gun and feeling depressed shortly after a fight with an ex-girlfriend.

As the days following the shooting unfolded, the public narrative became narrowly focused on mental health and gun laws and was largely concerned with how a mentally ill person could legally purchase an AR-15 when so many red flags were raised prior to the offense. This is an important question, but we must also acknowledge how a lifetime of ostracism may have been a major contributor to his decision to purchase a gun in the first place.

Cruz was an individual who felt that he essentially never had a home and never belonged anywhere. He may have felt that he had no one to turn to and therefore ruminated on his seemly endless suffering as a victim who was socially and romantically ostracized by everyone around him. At every corner, he received messages of ostracism, which can be difficult to make sense of even if you have the appropriate tools to do so.

Cruz embodies an individual who was deeply mired in the resignation stage of ostracism. Bouncing from school to school and being physically removed from various institutions eroded his ability to develop relationships, self-esteem, or a sense of belonging. While the individuals who rejected Cruz have every right to communicate their discomfort with him, Cruz, like Pagourtzis and many others, did not have the tools to cope with the cumulative effects of a lifetime of ostracism messages.

By engaging in the antisocial, aggressive act of shooting his peers, Cruz attempted to regain lost control while also seeking vengeance on those who made him feel unimportant. The romantic rejections that were communicated to Cruz prior to the shooting were certainly important pieces explaining his mental state at the time. As researchers suggest, ostracism messages can accumulate overtime, and the weight of these messages was too much for Cruz to handle as he was entrenched in the resignation stage of ostracism. This may not have been the driving force, but was certainly one of the contributing factors to Cruz's actions.

Marysville-Pilchuck High School Shooting

On October 24, 2014, Jaylen Fryberg concocted a plan to carry out a shooting at Marysville-Pilchuck High School, in a suburb of Seattle, Washington. Like Pagourtzis and Cruz, Fryberg's actions were premeditated; he targeted specific individuals, and a romantic rejection occurred a few days before the shooting. In contrast to Pagourtzis and Cruz, though, reports suggested that Fryberg had a strong support system of family and friends that cared about him and included him. He was even crowned Freshman Homecoming Prince by his peers. While this honor indicates a high level of popularity, Fryberg's social media posts and actions suggest that he still felt ostracized from desired relationships.

On the day of the shooting, Fryberg took his father's illegally purchased handgun and texted a group of his peers, including friends and cousins, to meet him for lunch at the school's cafeteria. He encouraged those who did not have his lunch period to skip class. After the students arrived, Fryberg got into a verbal altercation with his lunch companions before he calmly stood up and began shooting at them. It was the deadliest school shooting in the United States in 2014; four victims died instantly, while the others survived.

At some point the fire alarm was pulled, and panicked students ran in various directions while a history teacher attempted to disarm Fryberg. Before the teacher was able to subdue him, Fryberg turned his gun on himself and committed suicide. One of the survivors stated in an interview,

> I was in shock. I didn't know what to do. His face, it just looked so blank, and he looked so lost, you know? Like when you're staring at something for so long and you're just spaced out? . . . And after that first shot, you could tell he just needed to keep going. There was no turning back after that. (Kutner, 2015)

As investigators began to uncover the details of the events leading to the attack, they discovered that Fryberg and his girlfriend had broken up prior to the incident (Kamb et al., 2015). He sent her a text stating, "Ohk [sic] well don't bother coming to my funeral." The day after, he texted her again claiming, "I set the date. Hopefully you regret not talking to me. You have no idea what I'm talking about. But you will. Bang bang I'm dead." After she told him to stop, he responded, "No. You don't care. I don't care."

Fryberg also sent a photo of the handgun between his legs to an individual on social media, asking for them to call him before he did "this thing." Afterwards, he sent his father a text stating, "Read the paper on my bed. Dad I love you." He also texted family members of his funeral plans, "I want to be fully dressed in Camo in my casket" and to "Make sure all of my trust money or whatever goes to my brother." He sent another message to family members that said:

> "Apologize to [retracted] parents and tell them that I didn't want to go alone. And who would be better to go with then the one and only [omitted]. Also apologize to Andrews fam and [retracted] fam for me taking them with me. But I needed my ride or dies with me on the other side. I LOVE YOU FAMILY! I really do! More then anything. I needed to do this tho . . . I wasn't happy. And I need my crew with me too. I'm sorry. I love you."

Fryberg was a member of a respected family in the Tulalip Native Reservation (Carter, 2014). He was an avid hunter and had a close relationship with his family and heritage. Reports suggested that some peers at his predominantly white school witnessed him standing up to others who made racial remarks to him on several occasions. At one point, he was suspended from school after getting into a fight with a teammate because he was on the receiving end of racial slurs. While 56% of the student body is white, only 25% is Native American (Public School Review, n.d.), indicating that Fryberg and other Native American students could have been the targets of racism by some students. Unfortunately, reports did not go further into the details of these events.

Like Pagourtzis and Cruz, Fryberg was subjected to romantic rejection, but in his case, it was a series of romantic rejections. First, Fryberg was romantically rejected by Zoe Galasso. According to reports, Galasso turned Fryberg down when he asked her on a date. He subsequently found out that she had started a relationship with his cousin, Andrew. This experience was likely vivid in Fryberg's mind as he concocted his plan, because on the day of the shooting, he purposefully invited both Andrew and Galasso to the lunch table to execute them.

On Twitter, Fryberg indirectly communicated his anger towards Galasso and Andrew for dating when he tweeted, "Tell me what your plan is. . . . You can't make a bond with anyone like the bond me and you have right now. . . . Tell me what your going to do . . ." Fryberg's resignation and feelings of hopelessness chronicled in October were also preceded by angry tweets in September 2014 including, "Did you forget she was my girlfriend?" On August 20, 2014, he issued a warning by stating, "Your [sic] not gonna like what happens next!!" His tweets communicate the feelings of anger, hurt, and betrayal experienced during the reflexive stage of ostracism.

The second rejection occurred when, days prior to the shooting, Fryberg's girlfriend, Shilene, broke up with him too. The text messages to Shilene and his Twitter account both reveal a hurt individual who was deeply and negatively affected by the breakup. Fryberg tweeted, "I'm tired of this shit. I'm sooo fucking done!!!" on September 20, 2014. While Shilene had every right to break up with Fryberg and was in no way responsible for his actions, Fryberg felt betrayed and the pain and hopelessness of his failing romantic life were again communicated through social media and texts.

Chronic ostracism can lead to extreme antisocial aggressive behaviors (Baumeister et al., 2007; Twenge et al., 2001). Of particular relevance here is Williams's (2009) resignation stage in responding to ostracism wherein the target is excluded socially by others, they ruminate on feelings of inferiority and question whether their existence even matters to others. Though Fryberg was well-liked, had friends and was involved in social groups, his tweets reveal that the cumulative weight of the romantic rejections he experienced could have been a major burden for him to cope with alongside the racist taunting that he faced by some of his peers.

His tweets coincide with the mind of someone who was moving through each stage of ostracism and attempting to make sense of the threats posed to his sense of belonging, self-esteem, control, and meaningful existence. This can be deduced from Fryberg's apparent fear of dying alone. He purposefully murdered his friends so that even in death he would not be alone. In a final text to his family he stated, "I needed to do this tho . . . I wasn't happy. And I need my crew with me too. I'm sorry. I love you."

The Marysville-Pilchuck High School shooting reinforces our conclusion the communication of ostracism can have a significant impact on the mental states of certain vulnerable people. In the case of Jaylen Fryberg, he had many friends and family in the area, but his experiences of romantic rejection, racism, and social ostracism were cumulatively too much. He could not effectively manage the full scope of the messages he was receiving from his peers.

THE CASE FOR OSTRACISM AWARENESS

In the cases of Pagourtzis, Cruz, and Fryberg, reports revealed that they all experienced ostracism and interpersonal rejection events that had a deadly impact on their mental states before they carried out their crimes. Social media posts, text messages, and testimonials in news reports revealed a patterned progression through each stage of postostracism coping and the cumulative effects of many ostracism events.

When Jaylen Fryberg was rejected romantically and discovered that his love interest was dating his cousin, he took to Twitter in a way that closely mirrors the reflexive stage by conveying his shock, anger, and confusion. Also, in the reflective stage, targets of ostracism attribute their feelings of being excluded to others' actions in order to cope with the pain. Further, characteristic of the reflexive stage, Fryberg, for instance, chronicles his feelings of being left out and betrayed romantically by his friends through his Twitter account.

All three shooters also blamed others as the source of their pain. Finally, in the resignation stage, targets accept their status as excluded individuals and act out through pro- or antisocial behaviors in order to be noticed or regain control of their environment. In this stage, targets may have thoughts of suicide or self-harm (Chen et al., 2020). While Cruz had a failed suicide attempt prior to the Parkland shooting, Pagourtzis kept a journal chronicling his desire to commit suicide after his shooting, and Fryberg killed his peers so that he would not die alone when he committed suicide.

As society works to understand the antecedent conditions in which a potential shooter becomes a perpetrator, there is evidence that ostracism experiences are a significant contributor that requires further attention. The three shooters discussed above committed horrendous acts that damaged families, communities, and individuals forever. Yet, the questions linger as to why they would cause such irreparable harm and what can we learn so that we can prevent similar shootings from happening in the future.

These questions are at the core of investigations by students, families, administrators, news media, and law enforcement. In the quest for understanding, though, the public tends to focus on mental illness, access to firearms, or bullying as being primary motivators for school shootings.

In particular, bullying is sometimes used to explain all the negative communication that young people might experience, when being ostracized has the potential to be both more hurtful and less noticeable. While bullying tends to be communicated overtly, ostracism can be communicated unintentionally, covertly, with plausible deniability, and can exist without any verbal communication (Pelliccio & Nickell, 2018). The terminological differences between bullying and ostracism are not just semantic though; the lessons drawn from the differences in bullying and ostracism can help policy makers, school administrators, mental health professionals, teachers, and researchers focus on specific forms of communication that take place between interactants.

By giving more attention to the communication of ostracism and interpersonal rejection, we can see that there are many important factors at play that can allow us to reevaluate our assumptions about the antecedent conditions that foster school shooters. In doing so, we can reconsider what we view as effective support or prevention. In other words, we may think that spending money on antibullying campaigns is helping students, but in fact they are not, in part because they do not acknowledge ostracism as an important form of communication that can cause harm (Pelliccio & Nickell, 2018).

There are several important implications of giving ostracism more attention as a contributing factor to a school shooter's mental state. First, by studying the communication of ostracism in relation to school shootings, social workers and other mental health professionals can implement specialized support for those who are chronically excluded and be more aware of the behaviors and messages that communicate ostracism. Just as social workers, therapists, psychiatrists, and other mental health professionals tailor their treatment plans for each patient based on their past experiences, a framework for how to address chronic ostracism in adolescents needs to be as well.

Administrators can implement ostracism awareness programs that teach young people how to recognize the communication of ostracism, and how to cope with the experience through communication with others, as opposed to continuing to depend on antibullying programs which tend to ask audiences to stop bullying or to speak out against bullying behaviors (Pelliccio & Nickell, 2018).

Moreover, law makers can divert state and local funds for ostracism support networks. While social media can serve as a space where lonely individuals can make friends and communicate their emotions, networks specifically designed to connect ostracized youth and children can provide them with opportunities to better make sense of their experiences through the support of their peers and professional interventions.

Second, focusing on ostracism can also bring attention to the pervasiveness of ostracism messages in our everyday lives and how damaging they can be to adolescents under the right conditions. For example, instead of immediately attributing their child's negative mental state to bullying that can be overcome with time, families can acknowledge the pain of being ostracized and offer more effective support by communicating with their children. If this change in attitude toward ostracism is accomplished, ostracism communication will not be considered a "normal" part of the teenage experience that the young person just needs to get over, but instead acknowledged as a potentially serious source of difficulty that deserves further attention and communication.

Third, since social media is often a space where people express their emotions publicly, more attention needs to be directed at troubled students' social media usage. This does not mean that students should be policed, but rather that peers should have a way to safely report any concerns they may have to school administrators/officials, and that their reports be taken seriously.

For instance, one of Fryberg's peers showed a substitute teacher text messages in which Fryberg stated his plan to kill himself (Carter, 2017). There are disputes as to whether the substitute teacher passed on that troubling information to other employees or if employees and administrators took this information seriously. Regardless, allowing this information to slip through the cracks despite it being clear that Fryberg was a danger to himself highlights the need for students to be provided with safe, reliable mechanisms for reporting information about at risk peers to school officials.

Finally, and most importantly, by imparting ostracism awareness among adolescents and their families, we can better equip young people to cope with the feelings that come from receiving messages of ostracism. If young people are able to recognize ostracism communication and understand the process of sense-making that they will have to work through, then antisocial behaviors may be minimized. Such awareness can offer young people a frame of reference to better make sense of their feelings and to at least understand that their reactions are normal. Such ostracism interventions are only beginning to be studied, but as a society we can have discussions with young people about the effects and coping mechanisms of ostracism now.

The communication of ostracism can create serious negative outcomes for targets. Even though an individual interaction may seem minor, chronic ostracism can create a cumulative effect that makes individuals socially susceptible, unstable, and potential actors in antisocial behaviors. Ostracism can be communicated in a variety of intentional and unintentional ways, but every message exists in a chain of utterances and minor events can cumulatively deeply influence young peoples' mental states.

As society looks further into the conditions that foster school shooters and we try to make sense of these horrific acts, the communication of ostracism requires further attention by all stakeholders to begin offering effective and focused support for young people who are unable to cope with the weight of being ostracized. It is undeniable that mental health, gun control, toxic masculinity, and bad parenting are important conversations for us to have, but we believe the communication of ostracism should be included in that conversation as well.

REFERENCES

ABC News. (2018, February 20). Young woman claims she reported school shooter for stalking. YouTube. https://www.youtube.com/watch?v=A1LEprbmIow

Baumeister, R. F., Brewer, L. E., Tice, D. M., & Twenge, J. M. (2007). Thwarting the need to belong: Understanding the interpersonal and inner effects of social exclusion. *Social and Personality Psychology Compass, 1*, 506–520. https://doi.org/10.1111/j.1751-9004.2007.00020.x

Baxter, L. A., & Norwood, K. M. (2015). Relational dialectics theory: Navigating meaning from competing discourses. In D. O. Braithwaite & P. Schrodt (Eds.), *Engaging theories in interpersonal communication: Multiple perspectives* (2nd ed.) (pp. 217–229). SAGE Publications.

BBC News. (2018a, May 18). Dimitrios Pagourtzis: What we know about Texas shooting suspect. https://www.bbc.com/news/world-us-canada-44173960

BBC News. (2018b, February 16). Nikolas Cruz: Depressed loner "crazy about guns." https://www.bbc.com/news/world-us-canada-43067530

Benner, K., Mazzei, P., Goldman, A. (2018, February 16). F.B.I. was warned of Florida suspect's desire to kill but did not act. *The New York Times*. https://www.nytimes.com/2018/02/16/us/fbi-nikolas-cruz-shooting.html

Bethea, C. (2018, May 21). The Santa Fe shooting, "a dream I can't wake up from." *The New Yorker*. https://www.newyorker.com/news/news-desk/this-is-a-dream-i-cant-wake-up-from

Betts, K. R. & Hinsz, V. B. (2013). Group marginalization: Extending research on interpersonal rejection to small groups. *Personality and Social Psychology Review, 17*(4), 355–370. https://doi.org/10.1177/1088868313497999

Buelow, M. T., Okdie, B. M., Brunell, A. B., & Trost, Z. (2015). Stuck in a moment and you cannot get out of it: The lingering effects of ostracism on cognition and satisfaction of basic needs. *Personality and Individual Differences, 76*, 39–43. https://doi.org/10.1016/j.paid.2014.11.051

Burch, A. D. S., Robles, F., Mazzei, P. (2018, February 17). Florida agency investigated Nikolas Cruz after violent social media posts. *The New York Times*. https://www.nytimes.com/2018/02/17/us/nikolas-cruz-florida-shooting.html

Buss, D. M. (1990). The Evolution of Anxiety and Social Exclusion. *Journal of Social and Clinical Psychology, 9*(2), 196–201. https://doi.org/10.1521/jscp.1990.9.2.196

Carter, C. J. (2014, October 25). Washington state shooting: "Run, get out of here." CNN. https://www.cnn.com/2014/10/24/us/washington-school-shooting/index.html

Carter, M. (2017, April 6). Lawsuit: Marysville-Pilchuck teacher may not have passed on warning before mass shooting. *The Seattle Times*. https://www.seattletimes.com/seattle-news/crime/lawsuit-marysville-pilchuck-teacher-may-not-have-passed-on-warning-before-mass-shooting/

Carter-Sowell, A. R., Chen, Z., & Williams, K. D. (2008). Ostracism increases social susceptibility. *Social Influence, 3*, 143–153. https://doi.org/10.1080/15534510802204868

Chen, Z., Poon, K., DeWall, C., & Jiang, T. (2020). Life lacks meaning without acceptance: Ostracism triggers suicidal thoughts. *Journal of Personality and Social Psychology*. https://doi.org/10.1037/pspi0000238

Craig, T., Brown, E., Larimer, S., & Ballingit, M. (2018, February 18). Teachers say Florida suspect's problems started in middle school, and the system tried to help him. *The Washington Post*. https://www.washingtonpost.com/local/education/teachers-say-florida-shooters-problems-started-in-middle-school-and-the-system-tried-to-help-him/2018/02/18/cdff7aa6-1413-11e8-9065-e55346f6de81_story.html

Darrah, N. & Gaydos, R. (2018, February 15). Nikolas Cruz was living with Florida high school student in months leading up to shooting, attorney says. Fox News. https://www.foxnews.com/us/nikolas-cruz-was-living-with-florida-high-school-student-in-months-leading-up-to-shooting-attorney-says

Eck, J., Schoel, C., & Greifeneder, R. (2017). Belonging to a majority reduces the immediate need threat from ostracism in individuals with a high need to belong. *European Journal of Social Psychology, 47*(3), 273–288. https://doi.org/10.1002/ejsp.2233

Farr, K. (2018). Adolescent rampage school shootings: Responses to failing masculinity performances by already-troubled boys. *Gender Issues, 35*(2), 73–97. 10.1007/s12147-017-9203-z

Farr, K. (2019). Trouble with the Other: The role of romantic rejection in rampage school shootings by adolescent males. *Violence and Gender, 6*(3), 147–153. https://doi.org/10.1089/vio.2018.0046

Fernandez, M., Fausset, R., & Bidgood, J. (2018, May 18). In Texas school shooting, 10 dead, 10 hurt and many unsurprised. *The New York Times*. https://www.nytimes.com/2018/05/18/us/school-shooting-santa-fe-texas.html

Gonsalkorale, K. & Williams, K. D. (2007). The KKK won't let me play: Ostracism even by a despised outgroup hurts. *European Journal of Social Psychology, 37*, 1176–1186. https://doi.org/10.1002/ejsp.392

Kamb, L., Edge, S., Cornwell, P. (2015, September 3). Marysville shooter sent barrage of anguished texts to ex-girlfriend. *The Seattle Times*. https://www.seattletimes.

com/seattle-news/crime/marysville-shooter-sent-barrage-of-anguished-texts-to-ex-girlfriend/

Kelly, M., McDonald, S., & Rushby, J. (2012). All alone with sweaty palms—physiological arousal and ostracism. *International Journal of Psychophysiology: Official Journal of the International Organization of Psychophysiology, 83*(3), 309–314. https://doi.org/10.1016/j.ijpsycho.2011.11.008

Kerr, N. L., & Levine, J. M. (2008). The detection of social ostracism: Evolution and beyond. *Group Dynamics: Theory, Research, and Practice, 12*(1), 39–52. https://doi.org/10.1037/1089-2699.12.1.39

Kutner, M. (2015, September 16). What led Jaylen Fryberg to commit the deadliest high school shooting in a decade? *Newsweek*. https://www.newsweek.com/2015/09/25/jaylen-ray-fryberg-marysville-pilchuck-high-school-shooting-372669.html

Leary, M. R., Kowalski, R. M., Smith, L., & Phillips, S. (2003). Teasing, rejection, and violence: Case studies of the school shootings. *Aggressive Behavior, 29*(3), 202–214. https://doi.org/10.1002/ab.10061

McLaughlin, E. C. & Park, M. (2018, February 16). Social media paints picture of racist "professional school shooter." CNN. https://www.bbc.com/news/world-us-canada-43067530

Pelliccio, L. J. (2018). The process of ostracism message reception and meaning making. Wayne State University Dissertations. https://digitalcommons.wayne.edu/oa_dissertations/2123

Pelliccio, L. J. & Nickell, J. J. (2018). A critique of anti-bullying campaigns: How Neoliberalism, ostracism, and dissimilar definitions distort campaign rhetoric. *Iowa Journal of Communication, 50*(1), 120–148.

Perez, E., Morris, J., Ellis, R. (2018, May 21). What we know about Dimitrios Pagourtzis, the alleged Santa Fe High School shooter. CNN. https://www.cnn.com/2018/05/18/us/dimitrios-pagourtzis-santa-fe-suspect/index.html

Public School Review. (n.d.). Marysville Pilchuck High School. https://www.publicschoolreview.com/marysville-pilchuck-high-school-profile

Reich, S., Schneider, F. M., & Heling, L. (2018). Zero likes–symbolic interactions and need satisfaction online. *Computers in Human Behavior, 80*, 97–102. https://doi.org/10.1016/j.chb.2017.10.043

Rittenour, C. E., Kromka, S. M., Saunders, R. K., Davis, K., Garlitz, K., Opatz, S. N., Sutherland, A., & Thomas, M. (2019). Socializing the silent treatment: Parent and adult child communicated displeasure, identification, and satisfaction. *Journal of Family Communication, 19*(1), 77–93. https://doi.org/10.1080/15267431.2018.1543187

Riva, P., Montali, L., Wirth, J. H., Curioni, S., & Williams, K. D. (2017). Chronic social exclusion and evidence for the resignation stage: An empirical investigation. *Journal of Social and Personal Relationships, 34*(4), 541–564. https://doi.org/10.1177/0265407516644348

Sacks, B. (2018, February 15). The FBI was warned about a school shooting threat from a YouTube user named Nikolas Cruz in September. Buzzfeed News. https://www.buzzfeednews.com/article/briannasacks/the-fbi-was-warned-about-a-school-shooting-threat-from

Sommer, F., Leuschner, V., & Scheithauer, H. (2014). Bullying, romantic rejection, and conflicts with teachers: The crucial role of social dynamics in the development of school shootings—A systematic review. *International Journal of Developmental Science, 8*(1–2), 3–24. 10.3233/dev-140129

Twenge, J. M., Baumeister, R. F., Tice, D. M., & Stucke, T. S. (2001). If you can't join them, beat them: Effects of social exclusion on aggressive behavior. *Journal of Personality and Social Psychology, 81*(6), 1058–1069. https://doi.org/10.1037/0022-3514.81.6.1058

Van Zalk, N., & Smith, R. (2019). Internalizing profiles of homeless adults: Investigating links between perceived ostracism and need-threat. *Frontiers in Psychology, 10*, 350. https://doi.org/10.3389/fpsyg.2019.00350

Volk, A. A., Dane, A. V., & Marini, Z. A. (2014). What is bullying? A theoretical redefinition. *Developmental Review, 34*(4), 327–343. https://doi.org/10.1016/j.dr.2014.09.001

Williams, K. D. (2002). *Ostracism: The power of silence*. Guilford Press.

Williams, K. D. (2009). Ostracism: A temporal need-threat model. *Advances in Experimental Social Psychology, 41*, 275–314. https://doi.org/10.1016/S0065-2601(08)00406-1

Williams, K. D., Forgas, J. P., & von Hippel, W. (2005). *The social outcast: Ostracism, social exclusion, rejection, and bullying*. Psychology Press.

Williams, K. D., & Gerber, J. (2005). Ostracism: The making of the ignored and excluded mind. *Interaction Studies, 6*(3), 359–374. https://doi.org/10.1075/is.6.3.04wil

Williams, K. D., & Nida, S. A. (2017). *Ostracism, exclusion, and rejection*. Routledge.

Williams, K. D., & Zadro, L. (2005). Ostracism: The indiscriminate early detection system. In K. D. Williams, J. P. Forgas, & W. von Hippel (Eds.), *Sydney symposium of social psychology series. The social outcast: Ostracism, social exclusion, rejection, and bullying* (pp. 19–34). Psychology Press.

Chapter 3

Evolving Boundaries: Bullying, Online Intimidations, and Social Antagonisms

Brian M. Lowe

"The world's basically falling apart at this point and we're just in the middle of it."—Fiona, age 14

The mass shooting at Columbine High School in 1999 is now recognized as an historic moment of transformation in American understanding and perception of school violence. Not only were the number of victims killed and wounded unprecedented in American educational history, but the methods of the killers were also new in three meaningful ways: the killers had an attack plan to kill their peers and teachers indiscriminately, with weapons that they had gathered and improvised explosive devices that they had built, and they did so without a discernible motive to kill specific individuals.

The events of Columbine (the name itself is now shorthand for mass school shootings) spurred significant changes in social control in secondary schools with the objective of making them "harder" targets against similar attacks. These initiatives have included efforts to reduce the physical accessibility of school buildings and campuses, and the implementation of "active shooter drills" intended to prepare students among other things.

Columbine also spurred a persistent mythology about the causes of mass school shootings; that the shooters were both bullied and demeaned by popular cliques in the high school, and therefore the attack was an act of quasi-restorative revenge against those who had wronged them. In fact, as Cullen contends, there is significant evidence that both shooters had active social lives and were not the targets of sustained campaigns of bullying or intimidation (2009; 2019).

Cullen notes that this myth has persisted despite efforts to correct it. Cullen's finding is significant because one of the most frequently employed strategies in American secondary schools to pre-empt potential school shootings is to train school personnel to exercise vigilance for signs of intimidation, bullying or other forms of ostracism, as well as to encourage students to (self) report experiencing or witnessing anger or depression.

The transformation seen in schools has not occurred in isolation, as active shooter-incidents have become more common in the United States. According to the Federal Bureau of Investigation "Active Shooter Incidents in the United States 2000–2013" report, nearly a quarter (24.5%) were in "Educational" locations (both secondary and higher) and nearly half (45.6%) were in "Commerce" settings (Blair, 2016). Ames (2005) contends that the phenomenon of the mass shooter in school and workplace began in the mid-1980s in the United States.

BULLYING BEYOND THE CONFINES OF THE SCHOOL

As the introductory quotation from Liv suggests, concerns about school violence must be viewed from the perspective of profound social, institutional, and technological transformation. Just as secondary schools, colleges, universities, and commercial locations prepare for the possibility of an active shooter with the realization that there is no optimal security plan that will eliminate all threats, there is the growing realization that online intimidation in general is nearly impossible to contain as well.

Different vehicles for online intimidation (social media, cell phones, and multiplayer video games) are difficult to secure or police, and can also spawn broader social, political, and legal questions about what constitutes intimidation and what actions may be taken to contain and curtail such intimidation.

One significant consequence of the proliferation of various online communication platforms is what may be termed "extended adolescence." While this complex phenomenon has different manifestations, such as a decline in teenagers engaging in age-defined deviance like underage drinking, it is also characterized by weakened barriers between what are deemed "adult" and "teen" online activities, including playing video games and participating in social media (Stetka, 2017).

In the cases of social media usage, cell phones, and video games, rates of participation between those in their late teens and early twenties are quantitatively indistinguishable, further undermining arguments that clear delineations should be made between adolescents and young adults in terms of online behaviors.

In its more extreme manifestations, it should not be surprising that some mass shooters, such as Dylan Roof, who was 18 when he killed nine people in a Bible study group in the Emanuel African Methodist Episcopal Church in Charleston, South Carolina, in 2015, had been radicalized online in his late teens (Neiwert, 2017). Roof participated in online discussions involving white supremacy prior to his attack in Charleston, an attack that he explicitly stated was intended to spark a race war. While threats of violence at schools or other venues are not solely driven by racial or ideological animus, these cases do serve to raise the possibility that forms of online intimidation may serve to cultivate a milieu that does encourage violence in general.

Investigating the continuum of online intimidation, requires emphasizing some of the qualitative differences between a Weberian-style "ideal type" (Weber, 1978) of modern secondary school bullying and contemporary online intimidation in order to illustrate the location on that continuum that online intimidation may occupy. These include forms of harassment involving video games, both between individuals (as in the case of the suicide of Conrad Roy) and within larger organized groups. While the virtual locations and platforms of online intimidation are new, they also follow some previously identified characteristics, including the formation of status groups.

AN IDEAL TYPE OF BULLYING AND SOCIAL CONTROL EFFORTS IN AMERICAN SECONDARY SCHOOLS

"Bullying" in—latter twentieth-century American secondary schools was conceived as being comprised of five elements. First, bullying is primarily characterized as verbal, symbolic and/or physical interactions that either occur in face-to-face situations or through antagonistic communication (e.g., an insulting note given to the intended target).

Second, bullying occurs primarily on school grounds, including adjacent spaces like gyms and athletic fields; bullying may occur off-school grounds, but largely as an extension of what has occurred on school grounds.

Third, bullying occurs primarily in those spaces where agents of social control have reduced surveillance and disciplinary capacity, such as locker rooms. In secondary schools, agents of social control include adults whose professional role explicitly includes maintaining social control (teachers, staff, and administrators) and who wield formal power in these efforts. Staff who do not have explicitly pedagogical expectations (such as custodians) may also feel responsible for intervention and/or reporting bullying if it is directly or indirectly observed, as in the case of eliminating antagonistic graffiti.

Teachers can sanction students through a variety of formal disciplinary mechanisms, including detentions and recommending students for additional disciplinary action by administrators. Others, including peers and parents, may advocate for the imposition and/or reduction of sanctions. However, it is these professionals who wield the ultimate disciplinary authority to both define and punish what constitutes bullying.

Bullying is most likely to occur in locations where social control is either formally relaxed or in more liminal spaces. Teachers are expected to control classroom conduct, and to immediately sanction disruptive behavior, including bullying, that interferes with instruction or other pedagogical activities. Such expectations are relaxed in cafeterias, locker rooms, and other spaces where surveillance is more passive, and students have more expectations of agency. For example, in cafeterias, adult monitors allow students some freedom in choosing where to sit and engage in speech that would not be accepted in formal classroom settings. Likewise, hallways and other liminal spaces are more likely to be locations where bullying occurs because surveillance powers are weakened or overwhelmed, as in when classes change.

In response to such realities, access to these spaces is controlled; students may be sanctioned for being "tardy" if travel between classes occurs outside of an established and regulated time frame. Students generally require some formal permission, typically a "hall pass" in order to be in a hallway during an unsanctioned time. Bullying may also occur in areas adjacent to school properties, especially those areas that are largely unavoidable such as school-adjacent crosswalks and therefore are also under weaker social control. These spaces are also likely locations for other forms of deviance, like smoking, because of the decreased likelihood of being apprehended by adults.

Bullying occupies a paradoxical position in education because it is simultaneously perceived as deviant, inevitable, and perversely beneficial. As Merton (1968) distinguished between the *manifest* (openly stated and recognized) and *latent* (not overtly stated or recognized in its consequences or repercussions) functions of institutions, social practice or phenomena, bullying and intimidation may be recognized as having at least tangential value for students. School administrators take pains in order to both limit and respond to bullying, treating it as an unacceptable form of conduct and something that students should not have to endure.

Conversely, bullying is perceived as an unfortunate but inevitable behavior that emerges within schools that may offer its victims latent benefits. While school administrators will move against egregious forms of bullying, there is also the potential interpretation that bullying provides its victims with the latent benefits of preparation for life beyond secondary education through learning to manage interpersonal difficulties and conflicts.

Students who are too quick to inform teachers and/or administrators about bullying may be perceived as weak or unduly sensitive, and perhaps therefore less likely to be able to weather the future demands of higher education, employers, and co-workers. Those who can respond to bullying without recourse to authorities may be understood to have developed the skills necessary for peer conflict resolution in the anticipated future workplace.

BULLYING AS A MECHANISM FOR MAINTAINING ADOLESCENT STATUS HIERARCHIES

Previous sociological research has examined how status hierarchies play into adolescent acts of intimidation and how such acts may be perceived by social control agents like teachers. Chambliss's (1973) "The Saints and the Roughnecks" demonstrates the importance of labels applied to adolescent deviant behaviors. In his ethnography of "Hannibal High School," Chambliss observed two groups of teenage boys, the "saints" (the sons of middle-class parents) and the "roughnecks" (the sons of lower-middle class and working-class parents).

While both groups of adolescents objectively engaged in rule breaking behaviors within and outside of school (including cutting classes, underage drinking, and interpersonal violence), the reactions of social control agents were radically different. The actions of the "saints" were perceived as being indicative of "boys being boys," with the presumption that they will naturally abandon these behaviors as they mature and assume positions of middle-class respectability.

Conversely, the behaviors of the "roughnecks" are perceived as being indicative of their deviant natures, and not simple youthful exuberance, and therefore they are subject to significantly more severe sanctions than the "saints," despite the discernible equivalence of many of their actions. Therefore, perceptions of, and responses to, "bullying" in this context are likely to be influenced by the socio-economic standing of the parents of the teens in question.

Anderson's (2000) distinction between the behavior of adolescents in "decent" and "street" groups may cause confusion amongst social control agents. In his ethnography of inner-city Philadelphia, Anderson identifies two models of family life that effectively contend for adherence by adolescents.

> "Decent' families adhere to conduct and values that are generally aligned with the larger American host society, albeit favoring stricter adherence to norms about personal conduct, like punitively maintaining enforced nightly curfews. "Street" families generally abide by what Anderson defines as, "the code of the street", ". . . a set of prescriptions and proscriptions, or informal rules, of behavior organized around a desperate search for respect that governs public social

relations, especially violence, among so many residents, particularly young men and women." (pp. 9–10)

Due to the ubiquity of the "code" in inner-city Philadelphia, teens must dress and act as though they have internalized this code through displaying and/or defending certain physical status symbols and through demonstrating and displaying an apparent willingness and capacity to engage in violence. Anderson argues that an inability to produce convincing performances renders individual adolescents more vulnerable to intimidation and violence by others who seek to elevate themselves in the status hierarchy.

One driving complexity for social control agents (primarily teachers and police) is the difficulty in discerning which adolescents are enacting the code because they have truly internalized it, and those who simply adhere to its apparent normative structure in the hopes of avoiding violence and intimidation through what Anderson termed "code switching." The irony of this dynamic is that "decent" adolescents who attempt to abide by adolescent social norms may be perceived and sanctioned by social control agents as actually being deviant.

Milner's (1994; 2006) analysis of status and teenage status groups also demonstrates that, far from being aberrant or detached from adult society, their behaviors and perceptions reflect the realities of adult society. Milner (1994) contends that status is a resource that is both relatively inalienable (difficult to effectively remove or forcibly acquire, unlike material resources) and inexpansible (the greater the prevalence of an object or category, the lower its prestige).

Status relations can be maintained partly through the elaboration of status rituals that are created and/or initiated by elites and are subsequently followed by others. Historically, status relations have included courtiers adopting styles of clothing, dance or other forms of etiquette, and even languages in order to emulate the ruling group. Significantly, these forms of elaboration were often time and resource intensive, and therefore act as a form of boundary maintenance by effectively excluding those who do not possess specific skills, items or understandings that were deemed especially prestigious. Therefore, those who might acquire wealth or political power were unlikely to be judged as being authentic peers because they lacked the social and cultural capital.

In the case of teenage status groups today, labeling something as "cool," including musical genres, clothing items or technology, and words or phrases, allows high-status cliques to reinforce their position within high school status hierarchies. Some of these forms of elaboration included labeling specific words, phrases, or forms of generally accessible cultural artifacts (including television shows or music) as "cool," this also includes forms of material status displays whereby specific consumer items and/or brands would be deemed more desirable than others.

Unfortunately, such status elaborations also encourage forms of degradation, whereby some behaviors, objects, activities, and groups are identified as having lower status. Some of the status of particular items (like clothing or other consumer goods) may be partly driven by cost. Higher status items identified as such by high-status groups are more difficult to acquire and therefore more difficult to copy or imitate.

This difficulty in procurement includes specific student clubs or activities that are formally open to membership by all students, but in reality, become sources of prestige or exclusion. Gate-keeping or access to specific formal student organizations may be maintained through formal selection criteria (such as requiring that students "try out" for an athletic or dramatic organization), or more informally, such as the current officers of a club deciding who will be "invited" to join a group.

Within the larger social hierarchy of school, membership in some of these groups is inevitably perceived as more prestigious than others, thereby contributing to the relative standing of particular groups on a hierarchical social continuum. One mechanism that high-status groups use to maintain their position includes public demonstrations of contempt for outside individuals and groups, including stereotypical "bullying" by verbal or physical means. While these forms of status display and boundary maintenance may appear to be driven by the adolescents themselves, Milner's analysis indicates that these activities are emblematic of the economic and social forces within the wider capitalist American social order.

HOW ONLINE INTIMIDATION DEVIATES FROM SECONDARY SCHOOL BULLYING IDEAL TYPE

One of the analytical advantages of describing an ideal type of adolescent intimidation or bullying is that it provides a stark juxtaposition with online intimidation and emphasizes fundamental differences between the two. Online intimidation is not bound by the physical locale of schools or their adjacent spaces. Social media exemplifies what Giddens (1991) termed "disembedding"; that is, how social relations are "lifted out" of specific physical (and social) locations, spaces, and times.

Posts on Facebook or tweets on Twitter and phone texts can be sent and received nearly instantaneously, from mobile devices anywhere there is Internet access. The round the clock nature of social media has caused educators and some psychologists concern about the potentially deleterious impact of "screen time" on sleep cycles, even if online activities do not involve intimidation. Unlike the Secondary School Bullying Ideal Type described above, online intimidation does not offer its victims any true respite when they leave school, although the actions of adolescents in school may be curtailed by teachers during instructional time and schools may limit data and website access.

In online communication there is the potential for collective online intimidation by persons who may not even know individual victim(s). "Trolling" is defined as antagonizing "online by deliberately posting inflammatory, irrelevant, or offensive comments or other disruptive content" (Marcotte, 2018, p. ix). Online "trolls" may never meet or be physically proximate to their victims, and motives for participating in online intimidation may be opaque to their victims. Moreover, "trolling" may be related entirely to online activities, such as reacting to an online post, and have no relation to the (physical) existence of the victim.

This form of intimidation may be even more disturbing for victims than interpersonal intimidations because of its apparent anonymous and seemingly irrational motivations. Such uncertainty and detachment may heighten any existing concerns about the potential for physical violence, as these threats are not easily understood, or their specific sources identified and therefore least guarded against.

The regulation and restriction of physical movement by students and adults in secondary schools have increased dramatically across the United States since the 1999 shooting at Columbine High School. However, another consequence of the disembedded nature of social media and online intimidation is that socially sanctioned agents of social control, school staff, are significantly weakened in terms of their response toolkit. Unlike in the case of the Secondary School Bullying Ideal Type, those formally tasked with controlling and responding to disruptive student behavior have little to no control over what occurs on social media.

Non-educational online activities are notoriously difficult to segregate by age. Online platforms, including Instagram and TikTok, stipulate that users must be at least 13 years old, as required by the Children's Online Privacy Protection Act of 1998 in the United States. Snapchat launched SnapKidz for users under 13 and does not allow messaging, but otherwise does not uniformly limit access to portions of their platforms based on age. These formal restrictions are difficult to enforce, and evidence suggests that enforcement efforts by platform providers are rarely undertaken.

A 2016 survey of 1,200 persons between 10 and 18 years old found that, among those under 13, "78% were using at least one social media network, despite being below the age requirement," the most popular social medial platform being Facebook, with almost half (49%) claiming membership (Coughlan, 2016). The illicit nature of underage social media use suggests that these estimates are low. The same survey found that almost all those respondents 13 to 18 years old (96%) had a presence on social media platforms, including Facebook, Instagram, and Snapchat (Coughlan, 2016).

Another survey conducted by the Safer Internet Day initiative of 13- to 18-year-old persons reported that most users found their experiences on these platforms to be "positive," but also that "more than four in five had seen online hate," such as offensive or threatening language (Coughlan, 2016). These data indicate that nearly all American adolescents have at least some presence on and interactions with social media, nearly a majority of preteens are also utilizing social media, and that roughly 80% of the adolescents have at least witnessed some kind of online intimidation.

THE AMORPHOUS BOUNDARIES OF CYBERBULLYING

Patchin's (2020) summation of the 2019 Cyberbullying Research Center's survey of cyberbullying of adolescents in the United States reveals both underlying assumptions of what constitutes cyberbullying and some of the inherent difficulties in studying it. Their April 2019 nationally representative survey sampled "4,972 middle and high school students between the ages of 12 and 17 in the United States" via an online survey (Patchan, 2020).

This survey defined cyberbullying as: "*Cyberbullying is when someone repeatedly and intentionally harasses, mistreats, or makes fun of another person online or while using cell phones or other electronic devices*" (Patchan, 2020, emphasis in original). The survey indicated that nearly 40% of respondents (36.5%) claimed to have been cyberbullied at least once in their lifetime, with "Mean or hurtful comments online" and "Rumors online" being the two predominant categories.

Nearly a third of respondents (30.1%) claimed to have experienced "one or more" of the identified forms of cyberbullying at least twice. Threats of violence, "Threatened to hurt me through a cell phone text" (12.2%) and "Threatened to hurt me online" (11.7%) were less prominent, as were hostile sexual references, "Posted mean names or comments online about me with a sexual meaning" (12.0%).

Online intimidation based on ascribed or achieved characteristics, "Posted mean names or comments online about my race or color" (9.5%) and "Posted mean names or comments online about my religion" (6.7%) were less common, as were more concentrated attacks through online impersonation (10.1%) or being the target of a "mean or hurtful video of me" (71.%) or "mean or hurtful web page about me"(6.4%) (Patchin, 2020).

Perceptions of cyberbullying may not be as sound as these data from the Cyberbullying Research Center would suggest. D'Anastasio (2015) observes that the Cyberbullying Research Center is "the only institution primarily dedicated to internet harassment" and that longitudinal data about the prolonged impact of cyberbullying is lacking. Evaluating the quantity of the deleterious consequences of bullying including "decreased work performance, violent impulses, depression and changes in sleep patterns" may be problematic in the case of cyberbullying (D'Anastasio, 2015).

D'Anastasio (2015) observes three qualitative differences in forms of online intimidation that have, at least anecdotally, played roles in severe forms of online intimidation that have even resulted in suicide. First, the nearly or entirely anonymous nature of online behavior may weaken inhibitions about comments and facilitate the sharing of compromising or damaging information, known as "doxing."

Second, the online milieu facilitates forms of collective action, thereby "permitting trolls greater organizational abilities than your regular school bullies" (D'Anastasio, 2015) magnifying the scope and duration of intimidation. This perspective on cyberbullying emphasizes its disembedded and uncontained nature. D'Anastasio (2015) cites the experience of Katherine Cross, who was a target in the 2014 online harassment campaign that became known as "Gamergate." Cross stated that the disembedded nature of online intimidation made what she experienced online more intense than the bullying that she had experienced in her secondary schooling.

Further, "trolling" can quickly achieve its own momentum. Despite the measurable consequences of online intimidation, the capacity for social media and platform providers and law enforcement to address them is anemic. The quantitative amorality of the Internet is reflected in the fact that that "likes" are often prized more than of ethical conduct or creative achievements. Hardy (2016) notes that the online emphasis on "likes" and provocative comments encourages online attacks because they serve to elevate the status of the assailants receiving the most attention.

VIDEO GAMES AND AMBIGUOUS RATINGS

Even online activities that can accommodate age-grade segregation, primarily video games, have largely unenforceable age restrictions in terms of access to products and/or online game play. In the United States, the age classifications for games is primarily the purview of the Entertainment Software Rating Board (ESRB). The ESRB Ratings Process website states that an Advertising Review Council examines the advertising of video game manufactures in order to "ensure that correct and complete rating information is displayed on game packaging and marketing materials" and that "industry-adopted" advertising guidelines are adhered to. Unsurprisingly, there are age-related boundaries in terms of what kind of content is deemed inappropriate.

While there is consensus regarding the adult nature of the depiction of violence and drug use in gaming age restrictions, other themes are scrutinized in vastly different ways, as in the case of *The Sims 4*. In Germany, the absence of violence allows for its classification as appropriate for preteen players. In contrast in Russia, the choice to create residential same-sex couples in the game has earned it a classification as suitable only for adults (Robot, 2020).

Video games and their (social) uses are emblematic of the challenges in operationalizing online intimidation in that there is disagreement about what is age appropriate, the general weakness of age restrictions in excluding potential players by age, and the reality that game play is nearly as prevalent as social media use in the lives of teens.

Playing online video games is a common social activity among American adolescents. Lenhart (2015) states that "fully 72% of all teens play video games on a computer, game console or portable device like a cellphone, and 81% of teens have or have access to a game console." Critically, gaming is a very social activity, one that Lenhart contends is especially important for today's adolescent males as a vehicle for creating and maintaining friendships.

Lenhart, in the Pew Trust report "Video Games are Key Elements in Friendships for Many Boys" observes that, "more than half of teens have made new friends online, and a third of them (36%) say they met their new friend or friends while playing video games." Lenhart states that gaming may occur "both with others in person (83%) and online (75%). Teen gamers also play games with different types of people—they play with friends they know in person (89%), friends they know only online (54%), and online with others who are not friends (52%)" (Lenhart, 2015). Related to this phenomenon is that adolescent boys who play online/networked games are significantly more likely to play with voice connections that permit communication with others in the online match or session (81% of boys versus 28% of girls).

The social dimension to gaming is analytically significant because it both reveals how some online communication is conducted and how identifying authentic online intimidation may be problematic. One central element of online gaming-centered communications is "trash-talking" opponents during a match or session.

Lenhart's focus group participants indicated that "trash talk" ran the gamut from prolific profanity to threats of violence coming from teens and young adults. Despite the hostility, older teen players viewed this as part of gaming: "Older teen boys talked about how younger teens, in this case siblings, needed to learn how to handle trash talk in games. 'No, they have to do the same thing,' said a high school boy. 'It's for the game'" (Lenhart, 2015).

Lenhart's respondents suggest four qualities about conversations during game play. First, at least for boys, there is the general expectation that participants may be aggressive or antagonistic to some degree. Second, how these communications are interpreted is informed by the gaming activity itself, as one respondent noted that comments are simultaneously "harsh" and "funny." This observation is similar to Anderson's (2000) concept of "code switching" in that it might be difficult for third parties to accurately distinguish between typical game-play discourse and more significant threats.

Third, the disembeddedg nature of gaming parallels other forms of social media in that players may be involved with persons who are socially and geographically distant. Finally, like social media, there is no effective age segregation. Middle-school aged boys may be in the same match as young men in their 20s, and therefore subject to verbal comments that are viewed by young adults as simply part of game play but may be threatening to younger players. The apparent hostility expressed during video game play might be accepted by the participants as normal, and not as an actual threat to commit harm.

EVOLVING BOUNDARIES OF SCHOOL VIOLENCE AND THE DECLINE OF CERTAINTY

Whatever the limitations of the Traditional Ideal Type of intimidation and school-based responses to it, it allows us to identify two additional aspects of typical responses to bullying: an enforced consensus of *epistemological certainty* and *ontological security*. Teachers and school administrators have a significant level of agency in surveying and defining what constitutes forms of intimidation among students and responding to those acts in the name of maintaining social order in the school.

Such judgment likely never attains universal agreement among students, school staff, and the larger community but contribute to a spectrum of understanding of what kinds of disruptive activities would be identified, labeled, and punished as "bullying" or otherwise intolerable conduct. These conditions also indirectly recognize forms of "soft deviance" that might be informally sanctioned but not overtly punished. Such a normative consensus provides a spectrum of conduct with perceivable consequences ("If you do that, you're going to get a detention.") and provides a degree of ontological security within and outside of the school. Giddens (1991) contends that ontological security provides a sense of individual well-being and a shared sense of predictable continuity.

In the case of school staff identifying and punishing bullying and other forms of intimidation, there is a level of predictability regarding what kinds of behaviors are likely to be punished, and therefore a reassurance that those kinds of behaviors are less likely be encountered. Once the conditions of surveillance, identification and classification of behaviors are removed from the confines of the school and are placed in environments in which there is little age segregation or social control, a decline in epistemological certainty and ontological security is likely. This is exactly what has transpired in the digital milieu with forms of online intimidation.

The case of Sandy Hook is indicative of the decline of epistemological certainty and ontological security within the digital milieu. On the surface, the events of Sandy Hook appeared both shocking and incontestable. On December 14, 2012, 20-year-old Adam Lanza shot and killed his mother, Nancy, with a Bushmaster Model XM15-E2S rifle (a weapon legally purchased by Nancy Lanza). Adam Lanza then proceeded to the Sandy Hook Elementary school where he shot and killed 20 children and six adults.

The actions of elected officials following these killings were intended to provide some degree of epistemological certainty and ontological security, beginning with a visit to Sandy Hook by President Obama on December 16, 2012. President Obama described the event as a "tragedy" and called for the nation to unite and prevent such "intolerable" shootings in the future.

Subsequent reports from Connecticut stated (in 2013) that Lanza had acted alone and that (in 2014) the Connecticut Office of the Child Advocates reported that "warning signs" about Lanza had been missed. In sum, these actions by Federal and State officials made epistemological (this mass shooting was a "tragedy" caused by a lone killer that could possibly have been prevented if "warning signs" had been heeded) and ontological (these atrocities are not inevitable and must be prevented in the future) sense. Despite these efforts, and abundant evidence that the killings at Sandy Hook had occurred as documented in news media and governmental reports, alternative realities began to develop within the digital milieu.

The digital aftermath of the murders at Sandy Hook Elementary is an excellent case study in the evolution of alternate realities around this and other mass shootings. Within 30 days of the mass killing, "The Sandy Hook Shootings—Fully Exposed" appeared on YouTube and received over 10 million views (Spies, 2015). This video purported that the Sandy Hook killings were not, in fact killings, and the entire event was fabricated as a "false flag" intended to provoke a post–Port Arthur style effort to restrict firearms.

"Port Arthur" refers to a 1996 mass shooting in Port Arthur Australia that resulted in 35 deaths and 23 wounded, and was followed by the National Firearms Agreement that prohibited automatic and semi-automatic rifles and a buy-back program that acquired over 640,000 firearms (Grimson, 2016). Merlan defines the "false flag" motif as "the idea that mass casualty events have been orchestrated or carried out by the government to consolidate its power." (Merlan, 2019, p. 81)

The YouTube video was not the sole source of counterfactual interpretations. Infowars creator and host Alex Jones embraced and promoted the Sandy Hook as "false flag" operation, an initiative that contributed to his de-platforming in 2018 from YouTube, Facebook, and Apple (Tobias, 2018), along with retired school official Wolfgang Halbig. Jones repeatedly interviewed Halbig on Infowars, and Halbig independently promoted his claims that the killings at Sandy Hook were a hoax.

His efforts included the distribution of identifying information about Leonard Pozner, the father of Sandy Hook victim Noah Pozner. Subsequently, Pozner has been the target of online intimidation and death threats including the 2017 case of Lucy Richard, who was jailed for five months for repeatedly threatening Pozner, and as of this writing lives in hiding as a result of other online threats (Williamson, 2020).

Sandy Hook is not unique in being the subject of counterfactual depictions that challenge the reality of mass shootings in favor of an explanation that these events are fabricated and part of "false flag" conspiracies. The 2018 Parkland mass shooting also became the target of such a campaign, with student survivors including David Hogg quickly facing accusations of being "crisis actors." This accusation is especially jarring, because crisis actors do exist. "They are simply performers hired to play disaster victims in emergency drills or wounded combatants in military exercises. They provide a degree of realism for people practicing for real emergencies further down the line" (Wilson, 2018).

In the case of Parkland, many of the "false flag" claims were based on the emotional displays of students like Hogg as they were interviewed on television and perceived as somehow insufficiently authentic. These students were subsequently labeled by conspiracists as "crisis actors." Such accusations effectively negate the reality of mass shootings, in which the physical evidence, government and media documentation, and personal testimonies are dismissed as an illusion created for nefarious reasons (Baudrillard, 1994). Such accusations are not limited to school shootings; the 2017 shootings in Las Vegas, Nevada, and in Sutherland Springs, Texas, have also been contested as "false flag" events (Merlan, 2019; Neiwert, 2020).

Romance, Intimidation, and Suicide: The Case of Conrad Roy and Michelle Carter

The digital milieu can make the identification and categorization of interpersonal relationships more complex for third parties to gauge. The case of the suicide of Conrad Roy in 2014 emphasizes these ambiguities for parents and legal authorities. On July 12, 2014, 18-year-old Conrad H. Roy III died of asphyxiation from carbon monoxide in his pickup truck in the parking lot of a Kmart in Fairhaven, Massachusetts. Roy's apparent premeditated suicide garnered international media attention because of the innovative legal case that followed in its wake.

On investigating Roy's death, local police discovered that Roy had been in contact with 17-year-old Michelle Carter via text messages and one phone call during the night of his death and had shared scores of texts in the preceding days. This evidence was central to the case brought by the Bristol County District Attorney in charging Carter with involuntary manslaughter as a youthful offender in Roy's death, and resulting in an indictment by a grand jury on February 5, 2015 (Cohan, 2019). The subsequent 2017 trial resulted in Carter's conviction for involuntary manslaughter and subsequent sentencing to two and a half years in prison, a conviction that was upheld by the Massachusetts State Supreme Court in later appeals (Cohan, 2019).

The case of Conrad Roy and Michelle Carter exemplifies the liminal nature of adolescent digital relationships. The precise nature of the relationship between Carter and Roy was unclear, both in terms of their significance to each other and the fact that their relationship was almost entirely based on text messages.

While Roy and Carter met in Florida, most of their relationship unfolded in their respective Massachusetts communities, as noted by Lusky (2020), "Conrad Roy met Michelle Carter in Florida in 2012, while both were visiting relatives. Despite the fact that the two lived only 35 miles apart in the Boston area, they only met in person a few times, mostly keeping their relationship maintained through emails and texts." The nature of their relationship was also murky, as Taylor, K. (2019) observed: "their relationship was intense; they texted dozens of times a day. Ms. Carter spoke of Mr. Roy as her boyfriend, though he did not appear to regard her in the same way."

While their relationship evaded easy categorization, as they apparently did not share easily discernible interests, their relationship did have an intensity, as expressed through sometimes dozens of text messages sent daily. This ambiguity is explored by filmmaker and director Erin Lee Carr in her 2020 two-part documentary *I Love You, Now Die* (Wynne, 2019). The relationship between Carter and Roy becomes even more legally fraught because of their respective ages. While their relationship began while they were both teenagers, Roy was 18, and therefore legally an adult, while Carter was 17 and a minor at the time of Roy's death.

Finally, the mental health standing of both Roy and Carter further complicates the nature of their digital relationship. Roy had been diagnosed with depression, been a documented victim of a domestic physical assault, had previously attempted suicide, and had been receiving counseling at the time of his death. Carter had suffered from an eating disorder and had been prescribed antidepressants (Seelye & Bidgood, 2017).

Beyond the nebulous dimensions of their relationship, the fact that this tragedy became the subject of an innovative legal ruling and policy initiative is indicative of the evolving boundaries of online intimidation as potential sources of violence. Taylor (2019) notes that the evidence around what Conrad and Roy discussed in their texts does not meet the legal definition of a suicide pact which Taylor (2019) states is generally understood as two parties agreeing to commit suicide together (pp. 626–627).

The case of involuntary manslaughter against Carter rested on her persuasive encouragement of Roy's suicide. The texts that Carter and Roy exchanged just prior to Roy's suicide revealed that she not only had knowledge of his thoughts and plans, including acquiring the portable generator that would be used in his suicide, but she literally pushed him to execute his plan, "thinking you need to just do it. No more waiting."

In response to the legal ambiguities revealed in this case, Massachusetts Senator Barry N. Feingold and Representative Natalie Higgins introduced bill S. 2382, "An Act Relative to Preventing Suicide" in July 2019. This legislation was dubbed "Conrad's Law" in news reports (Levenson, 2019) and explicitly identifies "suicidal ideation," thinking about, considering, or planning suicide and its encouragement as a criminal act.

GAMERGATE AND THE EVOLUTION OF ONLINE INTIMIDATION

The events of 2014 that became known collectively as "Gamergate" is both a noteworthy event in the development of U.S. digital culture and in understanding the genealogy of online intimidation, how such intimidation can include threats of violence, and how boundaries between teens and adults are blurred in the digital milieu. Carmichael and Spanfeller's (2014) summary of the precipitating events of Gamergate suggests many of the behaviors associated with online intimidation, including threats of violence, became apparent in this case. Gamergate began in 2014 as attacks on video game designer Zoe Quinn and led to violent threats against several other women as well.

The events of Gamergate became a vehicle for Steve Bannon, then editor at the right-wing *Breitbart* website, for identifying how the anger and frustration unleashed in Gamergate could be harnessed by political causes. Both Bannon and Milo Yiannopoulos at *Breitbart* viewed the trolling online culture as being conducive to their cultural and political messages (Bernstein,

2017). Bannon and Yiannopoulos harnessed the hostility expressed on online platforms like 4chan and steered it towards their political objectives.

4chan was created by 15-year-old Christopher Poole in 2003 as a place where he and others could share their interests in Japanese anime and was subsequently colonized by part of what would become known as the alt-right. As Green (2017) observed, Bannon saw gamers—white males in their teens and 20s who understood trolling, gaming trash talk, and other forms of online intimidation—as an extension of the audience that Andrew Breitbart had hoped to win over to the political right with his online content.

Once Bannon gained control of *Breitbart*, he expanded his quest as "he envisioned a great fusion between the masses of alienated gamers, so powerful in the online world, and the right-wing outsiders drawn to *Breitbart* by its radical politics and fuck-you attitude" (Green, 2017, p. 146).

EVOLVING BOUNDARIES AND REINTERPRETING THREAT OF VIOLENCE

In his account of the Parkland mass shooting, Cullen (2019) notes that the killer was neither an avid participant or victim of online intimidation and had been expelled from Parkland prior to his attack. What made the Parkland attack especially noteworthy was its aftermath.

Many of the surviving Parkland students, assisted by their faculty, immediately engaged in social media aikido by using this event to bring attention to the tragic and solvable reality of mass shootings in the United States. "The Parkland kids seem to have accidentally solved the problem of celebrity shooters simply by becoming bigger celebrities themselves. It took David Hogg 24 hours to become the first survivor to surpass his attacker in fame. Emma Gonzalez went viral shortly thereafter. Meanwhile, the killer's name has already been forgotten" (Cullen, 2019, pp. 10–11).

Hogg, Gonzalez, and others from Parkland became the nucleus for the March for Our Lives, a multicity protest on March 24, 2018, which numbered an estimated 470,000 attendees in Washington, D.C., and "1.4 to 2.1 million people at 763 locations nationwide, plus 84 uncounted marches abroad" (Cullen, 2019, p. 207). Despite the focus on school shootings, only about 10% of the attendees were under 18 (Cullen, 2019, p. 208). Cullen also notes that in the weeks following the Parkland mass killing and related media coverage, students including Hogg and Gonzalez became the targets of online "trolls" and thinly disguised threats of violence (2019).

The experience of the Parkland shooting survivor-activists mirrors other examples of social media being deployed in potentially violent conflicts.

Patrikarakos's (2017) account that the roles of social media has played in contemporary armed conflicts, by both states and non-state actors, was built on the premise that these twenty-first-century conflicts point to the emergence of a new ontological condition for humanity, "social media has helped to dismantle traditional information and media hierarchies, and in doing so has given birth to a new type of hyperempowered individual, networked, globally connected, and more potent than ever before: a uniquely twenty-first-century phenomenon I term Homo digitalis" (p. 9).

The conflicts that he examines, including the Ukraine, Israel, and Hamas and the digital caliphate of ISIS (Islamic State), all involve the use of social media by both adolescents and young adults in both coordinating actions "on the ground" and promoting (counter) narratives that are favorable to their respective causes. Pomerantsev (2019) makes similar observations in his "adventures in the war against reality" while older persons, usually men, may be directing and financing differing forms of online intimidation, it is often adolescents and those in their early twenties who carry out these campaigns.

Pomerantsev (2019) describes a meeting with "P" in the Philippines, who "began his online career at the age of fifteen, creating an anonymous page that encouraged people to speak about their romantic experiences" (p. 4). At 16, he was "approached by corporations who would ask him to sneak in mentions of their products" and by "the age of twenty, he claims he had fifteen million followers across all platforms" (2019, p. 4).

While these accounts may seem distant from the concerns of violence and online intimidation in American schools, they do suggest more of a continuum between what may occur on social media, in video games, and through cell phones as they morph into larger episodes and campaigns of trolling, misinformation, and other forms of intimidation. The assumption is that there are qualitative differences between "traditional" bullying among secondary school students and forms of online intimidation. Traditional bullying often occurs in *liminal spaces*, those areas in schools where formal social control is weakened, and students have more agency to intimidate their peers, possibly motivated by maintaining their status in the students' social hierarchy (Milner, 2006).

As divisions between our digital and physical lives blur, policing deviant behavior is beyond the capacity of any single authority—school administrator, local authority, or platform administrator—to control, the opportunities for massed intimidation and threats of violence expand. Online intimidation easily transcends more microsociological spatial limitations, providing a context for relationships to exist outside of school or parental control.

The disembedded nature of texting, for example, allowed Conrad Roy and Michelle Carter to continue an intense relationship that only concluded with his death under circumstances so perplexing that Massachusetts is currently considering a law explicitly criminalizing active and virtual encouragement of suicide. While singular, this case is noteworthy in that it illustrates the difficulty in controlling (and even categorizing) digital communications and interpreting their nature and possible consequences.

As previously discussed, social media platforms have weak and poorly enforced age-restrictions, meaning that teens freely interact with each other, and with older persons. While such activities may be an increasingly central aspect of adolescent life, the capacity for any singular group to regulate online activities is at best a pale reflection of the relative control in the context of "traditional" bullying. This distinction is highlighted by the fact that there are discrepancies and disagreements among video games regulations concerning what the phrase "age appropriate" connotes.

The other difficulty with examining online intimidation is that it is difficult to assess the correlation between online activity and actual threats of violence. As previously noted, male adolescent online gaming likely will involve "trash talk," including profanity and caustic remarks. Third parties assessing online gaming exchanges may have difficulty recognizing variations of "code switching" as Anderson (2000) identified, and may therefore have trouble distinguishing normal game-play discourse from more pronounced threats.

This difficulty may become even more pronounced when the status dimension of online intimidation is factored in. An additional motive for making caustic and inflammatory comments might be made by those simply hoping to achieve more recognition from peers rather than to express sincere malevolence.

As Milner (2006) suggests in his analysis of high school status hierarchies, the way status relations are created and maintained bear strong parallels with similar practices in adult social settings. The most significant distinction between Traditional Ideal Type bullying and online bullying is that "trolling" or other forms of online intimidation can easily expand in scale and scope, leading a single individual to be the target of potentially hundreds or thousands of online attacks that may occur without warning.

As Ronson's (2015) account of Justine Sacco, a British woman who received over 100,000 hostile tweets in response to one she sent out to her 170 followers in less than 20 hours, indicates this is not hyperbole. Like the victims of Gamergate, Ms. Sacco had to physically relocate out of fear of violent reprisals.

The cases of Gamergate and other online actions that contributed to the growth of the "alt-right"also demonstrate that it is highly problematic to make a distinction between adolescents and younger adult men in these cases. Clearly the social rules for engaging in online communication is learned by users as teens; what is made of it will be of concern to all those seeking to cultivate digital civility. As social media platforms explicitly favor quantifiable attention (through "likes," etc.), and informally through attention paid to the most norm-violating "trolling," online intimidation is likely only to accelerate.

REFERENCES

Ames, M. (2005). *Going postal: Rage, murder, and rebellion: From Reagan's workplaces to Clinton's Columbine and beyond.* Soft Skull Press.

Anderson, E. (2000). *Code of the street: Decency, violence and the moral life of the inner city.* Norton.

Baudrillard, J. (1994). *Simulacra and simulation.* (S. Glaser, Trans.). University of Michigan Press.

Bernstein, J. (2017, October 26). Here's how Breitbart and Milo smuggled Nazi and white nationalist ideas into the mainstream. Buzzfeed. https://www.buzzfeednews.com/article/josephbernstein/heres-how-breitbart-and-milo-smuggled-white-nationalism

Blair, P. (2016, May 5). A study of active shooter incidents in the United States between 2000 and 2013. FBI. https://www.fbi.gov/file-repository/active-shooter-study-2000-2013-1.pdf/view

Carmichael, E., Spanfeller, J. (2014, October 14). The future of the culture wars is here, and it's gamergate. Deadspin. https://deadspin.com/the-future-of-the-culture-wars-is-here-and-its-gamerga-1646145844

Chambliss, W. J. (1973). The saints and the roughnecks. *Society 11(1),* 24–31.

Cohan, A. (2019, February 7). Timeline: Michelle Carter texting suicide case. *Boston Herald.* https://www.bostonherald.com/2019/02/07/timeline-michelle-carter-texting-suicide-case/

Coughlan, S. (2016, February 9). Safer internet day: Young ignore "social media age limit." *BBC.* https://www.bbc.com/news/education-35524429

Cullen, D. (2009). *Columbine.* Twelve.

Cullen, D. (2019). *Parkland: Birth of a movement.* Harper.

D'Anastasio, C. (2015). There is a lack of research on the longterm effects of cyberbullying. Vice. https://www.vice.com/en_us/article/d73eax/why-dont-we-have-real-science-on-cyberbullying

ESRB Ratings. (2020, June 6). ESRB Ratings. https://www.esrb.org/ratings/ratings-process/

Giddens, A. (1991). *The consequences of modernity.* Polity.

Green, J. (2017). *Devil's bargain: Steve Bannon, Donald Trump, and the storming of the presidency.* Penguin.

Grimson, M. (2016, April 28). Port Arthur massacre: The shooting spree that changed Australia's gun laws. NBC. https://www.nbcnews.com/news/world/port-arthur-massacre-shooting-spree-changed-australia-gun-laws-n396476

Hardy, Q. (2016, June 8). How gaming helped launch the attack of the internet trolls. *New York Times.* https://www.nytimes.com/2016/06/09/technology/how-gaming-helped-launch-the-attack-of-the-internet-trolls.html?searchResultPosition=3

Lenhart, A. (2015, August 6). Video games are key elements in friendships for many boys. Pew. https://www.pewresearch.org/internet/2015/08/06/chapter-3-video-games-are-key-elements-in-friendships-for-many-boys/

Levenson, E. (2019, November 12). Massachusetts lawmakers to debate "'Conrad's Law' to make coerced suicide a crime." *CNN*. https://www.cnn.com/2019/11/12/us/conrads-law-suicide-michelle-carter/index.html

Lusky, B. (2020, March 19). "I love you, now die": When young obsession turns dark. *Film Daily*. https://filmdaily.co/news/i-love-you-now-die/

Marcotte, A. (2018). *Troll nation: How the right became Trump-worshipping monsters set on ratf*cking liberals, America, and truth itself*. Hot Books.

Merlan, A. (2019). *Republic of lies: American conspiracy theorists and their surprising rise to power*. Metropolitan Books.

Merton, R. (1968). *Social theory and social structure*. Free Press.

Milner, M. (1994). *Status and sacredness: A general theory of status relations and an analysis of Indian culture*. Oxford University Press.

Milner, M. (2006). *Freaks, geeks, and cool kids: Teenagers in an era of consumerism, standardized tests, and social media*. Routledge.

Neiwert, D. (2017). *Alt-America: The rise of the radical right in the age of Trump*. Verso.

Neiwert, D. (2020). *Red pill, blue pill: How to counteract the conspiracy theories that are killing us*. Prometheus Books.

Patchin, J. (2020, February 3). 2019 Cyberbullying data. https://cyberbullying.org/2019-cyberbullying-data

Patrikarakos, D. (2017). *War in 140 characters: How social media is reshaping conflict in the Twenty-first century.* Basic

Pomerantsev, P. (2019). *This is not propaganda: Adventures in the war against reality*. Public Affairs.

Robot, M. (2020, February 19). Adventures in game ratings. *Kaspersky Daily*. https://www.kaspersky.com/blog/game-ratings/32492/

Ronson, J. (2015). *So you've been publicly shamed*. Riverhead.

Seelye, K. and Bidgood, J. (2017, June 12). Trial over suicide and texting lays bare pain of 2 teenagers. *New York Times*. https://www.nytimes.com/2017/06/12/us/suicide-texting-manslaughter-teenagers.html

Spies, M. (2015, December 16). What kind of person calls a mass shooting a hoax? https://www.thetrace.org/2015/12/sandy-hook-mass-shooting-hoaxers/

Stetka, B. (2017, September 19). Extended adolescence: When 25 is the new 18. Scientific American. https://www.scientificamerican.com/article/extended-adolescence-when-25-is-the-new-181/

Taylor, K. (2019, July 9). What we know about the Michelle Carter texting case. *New York Times*. https://www.nytimes.com/2019/07/09/us/michelle-carter-i-love-you-now-die.html

Taylor, S. (2019). Kill me through the phone: The legality of encouraging suicide in an increasingly digital world. *BYU Law Review, Issue 2, Article 10*.

Tobias, M. (2018, August 7). Why Infowars' Alex Jones was banned from Apple, Facebook, YouTube and Spotify. Politifact. https://www.politifact.com/article/2018/aug/07/why-infowars-alex-jones-was-banned-apple-facebook-/

Weber, M. (1978). *Economy and Society: An Outline of Interpretive Sociology.* Translated and edited by G. Roth and C. Wittich. University of California Press.

Williamson, E. (2020, January 27). A notorious Sandy Hook tormentor is arrested in Florida. *The New York Times.* https://www.nytimes.com/2020/01/27/us/politics/sandy-hook-hoaxer-arrest.html

Wilson, J. (2018, February 21). Crisis actors, deep state, false flag: The rise of conspiracy theory code words. *Guardian.* https://www.theguardian.com/us-news/2018/feb/21/crisis-actors-deep-state-false-flag-the-rise-of-conspiracy-theory-code-words

Wynne, K. (2019, July 9). "I love you, now die" Director Erin Lee Carr talks Michelle Carter case, surprising Feminist themes. *Newsweek.* https://www.newsweek.com/love-you-now-die-hbo-michelle-carter-erin-lee-carr-1448291#:~:text=Culture-.

Chapter 4

What We Talk About When We Talk About School Shootings: Framing the Stoneman Douglas High School Shooting in the Twitterverse

Ryan Ceresola

"Every day I hear someone slam a door or drop something loudly and my heart skips a beat for a moment. Not only am I now responsible for protecting my students against guns, but I am also responsible for finding every single warning sign, and making the correct decision every single time I try to help a kid I think is in emotional trouble. It is mentally and physically exhausting."—Eammon, graduate student & new teacher

On February 14, 2018, at 2:42 PM, the *South Florida Sun Sentinel* tweeted the first news about an unfolding tragedy: "We are hearing reports of a major police presence at Marjory Stoneman Douglas High School in Parkland." In the months that followed, citizens were captivated worldwide, both with learning about the devastation that led to the death of 17 innocent victims and by following the survivors in their quest to strengthen firearm regulations (Cullen, 2019).

The surviving students' message was clear: a concerted effort to convince Americans, especially young people, to vote for pro-gun control candidates and to advocate for legislation reforming gun laws. Powerfully, they called their campaign March for Our Lives, which appeared on Twitter as #MFOL (Cullen, 2019). Clearly, gun reform is one example of how the potential solution to the Parkland shooting was discussed and "framed"—that is, constructed and presented by the students. Simply put, frames are the ways people make meaning of the world around us, where objective realities (what happened) are provided with subjective interpretation (why it happened) (Borah, 2011).

The Parkland shooting was framed differently by different groups, however, and that framing has real-world implications, as messages about what should be done vie for public attention. To that end, this chapter asks and answers the following questions: What are the framed "solutions" that emerge in public discourse about the Parkland shooting? Who uses those frames? Which frames are most popular to the average citizen? And, perhaps most importantly, what does this mean for the real world of teachers, students, and activists today?

To answer these questions, one of the largest players in presenting real-time thoughts and comments from many Americans is examined: Twitter. This social media platform allows users to share their opinions, views about the world, and news stories in bite-size bits (280 characters is the maximum at the time of this writing), and has led to meaningful changes and conversations in the public sphere. From campaigns related to sexual assault reform such as the Time's Up movement and #MeToo, to the spread of misinformation related to COVID-19 and voting in the 2020 election, the discourse from Twitter influences the news cycle and public perceptions, and the messages and ideas presented online make their way through media outlets to the attention of nonusers as well (Pulido et al., 2020).

Twitter has introduced observers to new concepts, highlighted hidden worlds, and served as a repository of public sentiment for researchers globally. By analyzing the discourse on Twitter, activists, scholars, and advocates for reform can understand the frames that have emerged from the conversation about one particular event, the mass shooting at Marjory Stoneman Douglas High School, and use this information to better craft their own messages about what should be done to prevent future school shootings.

THE TWITTERVERSE AS PUBLIC SENTIMENT

Twitter (2020) states its major goal on the "about" page: to represent "what's happening in the world and what people are talking about right now." In many ways, it reaches that goal as politicians, public figures, and private citizens all have the ability to present their thoughts on virtually whatever issue they choose, within the 280-character limit.

Scholars have analyzed Twitter feeds in the past to search public sentiment related to as topics as diverse as coronavirus conspiracy theories (Pulido et al., 2020) to views on women's fertility (Micalizzi, 2020). Analyzing tweets is a useful method and particularly well-suited for this research, because the Parkland shooting was one well-documented online and the #MFOL students actively campaigned, and are still campaigning, on Twitter for much of their work.

This research consists of analyzing tweets related to the Stoneman Douglas High School shooting for notable themes and proffered solutions about what should be done about school shootings. To do this, the terms "Stoneman" and "Parkland" were searched for in six months of tweets after the event. The rationale for such generic terms was to parallel the general public's probable experience if they wanted to learn more about the shooting, but were not looking for something that already fit into a particular agenda. Just searching these two terms returned a sample of 91,293 tweets, indicating the widespread popularity of just these two phrases.

Upon creation of the sample, the ensuing analysis consisted of reading through tweets with one major question in mind: what does this tweet say *should have been* or *should be* done to have prevented this shooting or to prevent future shootings? Originally, all tweets were read that included the specific words "change," "reform," and "action," in order to observe the general sense of what people thought should be done. As tweets were read and coded for suggested solutions, a refined list of specific key words and hashtags that recurred in these tweets was generated, as shown in Table 4.1, and then tweets with those search terms were read and coded.

This process continued until no new themes emerged suggesting what should be done, thus reaching a saturation of ideas. The final sample culminated in 7,476 coded tweets, or 8.2% of the corpus of tweets (notably, 34% of *this* sample which consisted of news stories, with no opinions offered).

To answer the question of "which groups say what?," existing literature and emergent themes indicated which constituent groups were the primary "opinion-setters," and important groups to analyze in their discourse about the event. This included congresspeople, elected officials (the Presidential administration, the Florida state administration, and local Parkland politicians), student survivors and their families, local media (television, radio, and newspaper), National Public Radio, the National Rifle Association, Fox News, and general users. All tweets by each member of the first seven groups were read to further examine emergent themes, and no new themes emerged in this phase. Finally, elected officials and congresspeople were coded for political affiliation.

Supplementary analyses not shown here were also conducted, and significant differences were found in both constituent groups and the amount they tweeted certain themes, as well as political party the amount they tweeted certain themes (both at $p<.001$). Where there are statistically significant gaps in how much a theme is *observed* in a group compared to what would be

Table 4.1. Key Words and Hashtags Searched

Key Words	Hashtags
Thoughts	#mentalhealth
Prayers	#mentalillness
Heart (i.e., "goes out" or "is with")	#guncontrolnow
Mental	#gunreformnow
Health	#EnoughisEnough
Ill	#votethemout
NRA	#TeachersWithGuns
Gun	#guncontrol
Weapon	#StopSchoolViolenceAct
Amendment	#armingteachersgreat
Action	#studentsstandup
Reform	#standwithstudents
Safe	#Nomorethoughtsandprayers
Change	#endgunviolence
Policy	#thoughtsandprayers
Stop School Violence Act	#gunssavelives
Moment of Silence	#impeachtrump
Never Again	#prayfor
Assault Weapon Ban	#2A
Red Flags	#NeverAgain
	#Defendthesecond
	#assaultweaponsban
	#MFOL

expected if there were no influence of group membership is noted in the text of the discussion.

Finally, analyses to explore which tweet themes were most widely "liked" and retweeted by other Twitter users are presented in the final subsection of this chapter. With this methodology, this research aims to provide a relatively reliable and valid accounting of the most relevant themes related to framing the Stoneman Douglas shooting.

WHAT WE TALK ABOUT WHEN WE TALK ABOUT SCHOOL SHOOTINGS

Broadly, there were five major categories of tweets: gun reform, thoughts and prayers, standing with students, blaming, and mental health. These categories can best be described as "vocabularies of motive" (Mills, 1940): socially accepted rationales and reasons for something to have occurred. The themes, with notable subthemes, are presented in Table 4.2.

Table 4.2. List of Categories of Tweets Related to Parkland Shooting (n = 7,476)

	%	N		%	N
Gun Control	28.3	2,116			
Gun Reform	25	1,871	STOP School Violence Act	1.6	120
NOT thoughts and prayers	1.7	125			
Thoughts and Prayers	12.8	956			
			General Safety	0.9	69
Thoughts and Prayers	6.3	467	Law Enforcement Support	0.9	66
"Do Something"	4.3	321	Ceremonies of Remembrance	0.4	33
Standing with the Students	11.4	851			
Blaming	8.5	437			
Politicians Failed	3.5	261	Media Is Failing	0.9	69
The School/Law Enforcement Failed	3.0	224	Students Are the Problem	1.1	83
Mental Health Reform	5.2	392			
Mental Health	3.2	242	NOT gun control	2.0	150
Unrelated/News Stories	33.8	2,524			

Gun Reform

The largest selection of tweets was about the most tangible topic related to this issue: gun control, gun reform, and specific legislation that calls for curtailment (at least in some ways) of gun ownership. Over a quarter of tweets in this sample (28.3%) support the idea of gun control in some way, ranging from simply stating that guns are the problem to pushing for specific reform.

For the most part, these tweets' recommendations range from a general "gun control" to specific assault weapons ban, but the main message was that school shootings will not stop until gun laws change. For instance, one user writes:

> Gun violence is not a Sandy Hook issue. It's not a Parkland issue. It's an American issue. The threat of gun violence needs nationwide action. #GunControlNow #Everytown. This cannot wait for the next election. We need action today.

This statement articulates that guns and the violence they cause led to the Parkland shooting, the Sandy Hook shooting, and are a national threat. The user furthers the message with the popular hashtag #GunControlNow. These tags work to build a certain worldview of reality: browsers can log on to Twitter, search by hashtag, and see a multitude of messages all framing the shooting in the same way. General users were significantly more likely to use this frame than any other group in the sample, with 32% of their tweets being about gun control or reform—four percentage points higher than the sample's average.

A major player in emphasizing gun reform was the students themselves who used Twitter to convey their messaging quickly and concretely: a double-barreled agenda that young people should vote and for gun control legislation (Cullen, 2019). Often, these sentiments were some of the most well-reasoned tweets regarding the issue. For instance, one student said:

> The NRA does help educate gun owners, that's good however they need to do more. The bad part is when they actively lobby again things like Parkland #1 (HR4240) Universal Background Checks. But don't lobby to make it federal law that all guns are sold with trigger locks.

By using such popular hashtags as #NeverAgain and #MFOL (March for our Lives), the students set the agenda early and often (Cullen, 2019), and simultaneously create a shared view of the world with their followers. Notably, the survivors were largely successful in promoting their messages: on average, survivors saw about 860 retweets and 3,600 likes from their fellow users, both of which are significantly different ($p < .001$) from the average number of likes and retweets for the sample as a whole (140 retweets and 475 likes, respectively).

Importantly, there are political differences related to the relative frequency of tweets about gun reform. Democrats are much more likely than Republicans to call for gun reform or sensible gun measures. If there were no effect of political affiliation on the number of tweets related to gun control, about 75% of the pro-gun control tweets in the sample would come from Democrats and 25% would come from Republicans—instead 95% of tweets related to gun control come from Democrats and only 5% come from Republicans ($p < .001$).

Even the tone of the messaging from Democrats to Republicans is markedly different. For example, a Democrat Representative tweeted:

> All options must be on the table to include comprehensive background checks, bump stock ban, prohibiting the sale of military assault weapons and full

funding for gun violence research in a comprehensive manner that could have prevented the #Parkland tragedy.

This tweet advocates many options for gun reform legislation, constructing an image that the current status quo needs to be altered and that "all options" should be open for discussion.

On the other hand, in the few tweets related to gun control from Republicans, they do much less in terms of specifically mentioning the damage guns can do, often advocating for the (as of this writing still pending in Congress) STOP School Violence Act—a proposed law from Florida Representative John Rutherford, a Republican. The STOP act emphasizes early interventions (including some mental health checks) over gun control to encourage school safety, though the proposal does allow for gun control measures.

In one tweet, a Republican senator described STOP as "a historic investment in school safety and early intervention programs to stop violence in schools before it happens." This messaging, while in support of a bill that would provide grants to schools to use as they see fit, including installing measures such as metal detectors, focuses on vague language such as "safety" and "stop[ping] violence," rather than calling out for the need for gun control explicitly.

Emphasizing gun control and gun reform is the most popular way to frame the agenda related to school shootings on Twitter, and is mainly framed by general users, survivors of the tragedy, and Democrats. If Twitter's website is correct in that it represents real people's viewpoints, then the viewpoint of the majority is clearly articulated here.

Thoughts and Prayers

The next largest group of tweets, with about 13% of the sample, are those that convey condolences, sympathies, and heartbreak, but do not provide insight into the tweeters' conception of what *should* happen next: labeled here as "thoughts and prayers." Examples are typically short and to-the-point, including the following three:

> *General User:* Deeply saddened for those who lost their loved ones in #ParklandSchoolShooting. Prayers & thoughts are with everyone affected by this tragedy.

> *General User:* Thoughts and prayers to those affected in Parkland, Florida. This is so sad and happens far too often.

> *Republican Senator:* Absolutely tragic murders at Marjory Stoneman Douglas High School in Parkland, FL. Action must be taken. My thoughts and prayers are with the family & friends of all the victims.

While the wording varies, the specific tweets in this camp primarily focus on the sympathy of the writer, encouraging those facing this difficult situation, but stopping short of advocating for policy reform.

In the latter most tweet above, stating that "[a]ction must be taken" highlights a notable subtheme in this section. Just over 4% of tweets offer sympathy for Parkland, but then simply state something to the effect of "somebody should do something." This subtheme is categorized by mentioning the need for "change" without specific reforms. For instance, two users state:

> *General User:* If it can happen in Parkland, Florida it can happen anywhere in this country. #NeverAgain

> *General User:* This time must be different #ThisTime #NeverAgain #Parkland.

As in the tweet from the Republican Senator, these messages convey a sense of a desire for change, and speak strongly (e.g., "This time must be different" or the use of #NeverAgain), but no specific reform is proffered. In terms of constituent group differences, elected officials are nearly twice as likely as the general sample to offer thoughts and prayers (11% vs. 6%), and compared to Democrats, Republicans are much more likely to do so as well (25% vs. 6%). Thoughts and prayers are also tweeted at higher levels than would be expected for Republicans and for elected officials, indicating that signifying solidarity but not solutions might just be more politically palatable for these groups.

Relatedly, about 2.2% of the tweets emphasized general "promotions of peace"—calls for general safety, support for law enforcement and first responders, and mentions of ceremonies of remembrance for the Parkland families. These tweets fit into the "thoughts and prayers" category, as they do not promote an agenda for change, offer sympathy and support, and emphasize the benefits of the current political and governance system. For instance, some users tweeted messages of gratitude for law enforcement and first responders, such as one writing:

> In this dark hour for Parkland, we also witnessed the best of their town, w/police officers, first responders, & other great civilians w/selfless instincts, stepping up to respond, lead, aid, & heal.

While in some ways it is laudable to comment on the positives that emerge from the Parkland shooting, it also removes focus from potential solutions to the issue. In short, if these statements convey that citizens can generally count on social services to "step up" in times of tragedy, then it removes the impetus for changing the circumstances that led to such events.

Here is another large discrepancy between general users and political officials. General users tweeted support as about half a percent of their overall tweets, while elected officials promoted law enforcement as about 7% of their overall tweets. Further, 10% of tweets from Republicans promoted these groups, whereas only 1% of Democrats' tweets did. Both of these are statistically significant gaps, indicating the influence of group membership.

Relatedly, many elected officials used their position to mention remembrance ceremonies. For instance, Florida's Governor Rick Scott tweeted:

> I have proclaimed February 14th as Marjory Stoneman Douglas High School Remembrance Day in Florida. Tomorrow marks 17 days since the tragic shooting & I encourage all Floridians to join me for a moment of silence at 3 PM to honor the seventeen lives lost.

In this way, these tweets call to remember and honor those whose lives were lost, but they do not encourage meaningful reform. Elected officials are significantly more likely to tweet messages about ceremonies of remembrance than the general sample as well (7% vs. .5%).

Notably, the sentiment of "thoughts and prayers" proved particularly problematic for many on Twitter. Just under 2% of the entire sample condemned these types of tweets, particularly when these are the messages from the politicians. As one user wrote, "I'm sick and tired of the phrase thoughts and prayers. We need action." While this user's tweet is similar to the "something must be done" sentiment above, this user tacitly constructs the message that simply offering support is not enough to make real change—and, in fact, they are "sick" of such a sentiment.

Thus, the anti-"thoughts and prayers" frame is the idea that gun law reform cannot coexist with "thoughts and prayers." Tweets in this camp suggest that using the 280 characters to share sentiment undercuts the writer's ability to use the characters to advocate meaningful change. In this challenge to the thoughts and prayers focus, the user above indicates that these generalities deflect public outcry and avoid taking concrete action. In other words, when people focus their limited word count on consolations, or say something to the effect that "now is not the time to be political," it does not allow room to progress towards concrete change.

In line with this, others were more specific about *who* they found distasteful and *what* they desired. Overall, "anti-thoughts and prayers" tweets aligned with gun reform, though there were substantial attacks on the political process in these tweets as well. As one user writes:

> We don't need the prayers and thoughts of @RealDonaldTrump and the @GOP We need action. Get your hands out of the @NRA pockets. We need gun control and laws to help prevent this sort of atrocity. #Parkland.

Put more succinctly by another user, "Thoughts and prayers won't stop a speeding bullet. It's time for sensible gun laws." Notably, this backlash very much comes general users: of the 125 tweets coded as anti-thoughts and prayers, 122 of them were from general users—indicating that this sentiment does not trickle down from elected officials nor media agencies, but is something general users themselves articulate.

In sum, while some users denounced this frame, many others offered their support and sympathy: "thoughts and prayers" tweets cast the shooting in a light that offering condolence with no call for action. Feelings of sadness, of "hearts going out," and some sense of a desire to change are often stated, but the emphasis is not on tangible outcomes.

Standing with Students

As mentioned, one of the most compelling elements of the aftermath of the Stoneman Douglas shooting was the reaction of the students. A strong contingent of Stoneman Douglas student activists—and students at schools around the country—promoted voter drives, organized large-scale marches, sit-ins, walk-outs, and a variety of peaceful protests (Cullen, 2019). Messages "supporting the students" received large-scale support from Twitter, with just over 11% of all tweets in this camp.

These tweets explicitly spoke out for heroism and vigilance of the students in their fight to not be victims but instead political actors, often referring to the students as "brave," "strong," or "passionate." For instance, one user wrote:

> The March For Our Lives event in Parkland was inspirational. The students spoke with passion and have created a #NeverAgain movement that is changing our world. Thousands peacefully marched and remained respectfully silent when passing Marjory Stoneman Douglas. #MSDStrong

This message encourages students in their efforts to change the status quo, but does not necessarily focus on the message of the students—that of gun control. As another user stated:

> I can't march today but for those of you who are, I am with you in spirit and my heart. Proud of the Parkland students for making their voices HEARD and carrying so many others with them. #NeverAgainMSD.

Notably, this messaging is used particularly often by members of Congress, who are about twice as likely as the general user base to say that they stand with the students (25%t vs. 11%). In line with this, Democrats are five times as likely as Republicans to tweet their support and solidarity with the students.

This might be a politically savvy move, as politicians align with a progressive cause in a somewhat "safe" manner, because many statements of support do not directly state what the students are advocating. For instance, one Republican Representative tweeted:

> The devastating shooting in Parkland, Florida took place exactly one month ago & today, students walked out of class in an unprecedented demonstration. To the students marching today & the students I've met with in #IN05: We are listening.

This emphasizes the good work of students, offers a pledge to "listen," but does not commit to tangible next steps. In this way, politicians ride the razor's edge to "support the students" without supporting their policy reform demands.

The overarching message in these tweets is not necessarily one of calling for a specific reform per se, but instead supporting students in general. While some tweets mentioned *what* the students were campaigning for, the overarching emphasis of these tweets was not on the reform but the "young patriots" rallying and contributing to the democratic conversation.

Blaming

The penultimate grouping of tweets can best be described through the concept of blaming: where individuals do not state what specifically should be done but instead blame certain organizational failings. Broadly, 8.5% of tweets cast blame on politicians, the local Parkland police, Stoneman Douglas High School, or the media.

First, about 3.5% of the sample consists of tweets that blame politicians for a variety of reasons, with most stating that politicians are not doing enough to change laws. The major arguments are that politicians are in the pocket of the NRA, or that the process moves too slowly to enact meaningful change. For instance, a group called Florida Democrats tweeted:

> House Republicans had an opportunity to show they stand with Parkland Students, instead of the gun lobby. But, once again, they have decided that

protecting our children isn't their number one priority by voting against @CarlosGSmith amendment to ban assault weapons. #NeverAgain.

While this tweet is somewhat unique in that it calls for a particular action, most "blaming" focuses less on what specifically needs to change, and more on calling out elected officials for not doing enough to make *any* meaningful change. As one Democratic Representative tweeted:

Trump looked Parkland students in the eye & promised not to bow to the @NRA. Yet behind closed doors he sold out to the gun lobby like so many other Republicans in Washington. His reversal is disgraceful but sadly not surprising. This is what a reality TV presidency looks like.

Once again, the character limitation of Twitter provides a way to infer what people find the most important to share with their followers. Using the framework of blaming politicians provides a sense of where this Representative thinks the *real* power lies; that is, who is most responsible for changing the system. This exemplifies how framing helps to simultaneously convey and construct one's worldview on a particular issue.

As Spector and Kitsuse (2001, p. 73) argue, social problems are a "kind of activity" as opposed to "a kind of condition" and must be brought to the public's eye in a specific way before they are considered social problems. Framing this issue as related to political *inactivity* is a clear example of users constructing a world where politicians need to change the way they go about protecting citizens.

Somewhat ironically, congresspeople themselves were the most likely group to tweet messages stating blaming the political system, as this theme appeared in 7.5% of congresspeople's tweets (compared to 3.5% in the sample as a whole). Further indicating that this message is influenced by political membership, 11% of the tweets by Democrats in the sample challenged politicians, while no Republicans did.

What might help us understand this phenomenon? Perhaps it is that during 2018, in the months subsequent to the shooting, the Presidential administration was Republican, and both the House and the Senate were held by Republicans as well. Calling out the ineffectiveness of leadership is a particularly resonant vocabulary of motive in American society (Mills, 1940), as the Democratic process presupposes that individuals will call for change when they see fit. For Democrats, by virtue of not having the political capital to make major changes without Republicans' assistance, calling out a failing political body puts them in a position to demand change without admitting their own complicity in the governmental inaction that they say could have contributed to this shooting having happened.

Next, 3% of tweets decried law enforcement agencies or Stoneman Douglas High School itself for failing to move quickly enough to stop the shooting. Notable trends here suggested that both institutions failed to follow up on tips about the killer's likelihood of an attack or that police officers did not enter the building quickly enough during the shooting. For example, a Republican Representative tweeted:

> We need to ask tough questions and hold people accountable for the numerous breakdowns that led to the Parkland shooting.

Tweets in this camp also pointed to school officials for not reporting the killer to local authorities sooner for his disturbing behavior. In all, these messages convey that a great deal "went wrong" in how the shooter was handled before the actual event, and simultaneously deflect from other potential solutions such as gun control or legislative change.

"Blaming" these institutions was a particularly common tactic for Fox News as well as the NRA and its affiliates. Fully, 20% of tweets from Fox News in the sample and 44% of tweets from NRA advocated a line of argument that said, at least in some way, that the police or the school failed. Comparing that to the 3% in the overall sample shows a striking contrast in worldview for these organizations. In this way, Fox News and the NRA promote a frame of fear, where those who are supposed to take care of the rest of us do not.

There is little difficulty in drawing the connective tissue here: one organization wants people to stay tuned to its news and the other organization wants more people to buy guns (presumably for self-protection). As Benford (1997) argues, analyzing a group's framing allows us to understand their worldview: When the NRA and Fox News promote a world of fear as their central frame, they encourage viewers to blame organizational failings, and to listen to themselves as trusted authorities.

Lastly, just under 1% of tweets argued that the media portrays an inaccurate picture of the shooting, that will do nothing to make meaningful change. These tweets mainly fall in line with pointing out a liberal bias in the mainstream media. NRATV, for instance, tweeted:

> @CNN the network that led the debate over the Parkland massacre and ensured that it was anything but a debate just keeps offering up new examples of their total devotion to the donkey. But don't worry everyone. The hourglass turned, the sand ran out, their #TimesUp.

Some tweets in this camp decried media pundits like conservative political commentator Tomi Lahren for attacking the victims of Parkland, though the majority challenged the media's framing of the issue as one of gun control. Understandably, then, the NRA and its affiliates are the group with the highest percentage of their tweets attacking the media: fully 19% of their tweets do so, compared to the overall average of 9%, a substantial and significant difference. Once again, by explicitly framing the situation that media outlets are untrustworthy, the NRA implicitly states that people should look to them as a trusted source.

Interestingly, no tweets in this sample called out the killer himself without linking to an agency that "should have been" responsible for the individual's actions. As one user writes:

> While the alleged shooter may have had several issues, he also lived in a society where @GOP Sen. @marcorubio refuses to take responsibility for the role #gunculture may have played in this tragedy. @cameron_kasky at @CNN.com @NeverAgainMSD #neveragain #Parkland.

Once more, we see Mills's (1940) vocabularies of motive in play. In broader society, the mainstream media, and the Twitterverse, mass shootings are talked about typically as a societal failing (and not an individual failing), and so tweets that blame an individual, rather than an agency, for actions are seldom used.

In all, these tweets spend their limited character count to blame others for not "doing more," but seldom state reform efforts (though there are some exceptions). Instead, these tweets emphasize the negative actions of agencies "in charge" of preventing such a shooting. The theme of blaming deals not so much with solutions, but the problems of politicians, police, schools, and the media.

Mental Health

Finally, given the prevalence of conversation about mental health reform as a solution to school shootings and other gun violence in public discourse, it is surprising to see so few people arguing for mental health reform in the Twitterverse—only about 5% of the sample suggest that "mental health" is to blame for the shooting. These tweets state that the mental health struggles faced by the killer caused violence, arguing that more needs to be done to address deficiencies in our mental health care system in the United States as the primary solution to this problem.

The conversation around mental health is mainly directed at the concepts of "red flags" and "support services." As one general user stated:

> Speaking at the NRA's annual meeting, Trump said there "has never been a case where more red flags have been shown" than in the Parkland shooting.

By virtue of presenting "red flags" as a warning sign to be heeded and reported, these tweets emphasize that the killer's actions and mental stability should have been policed better. Importantly, this message was reported to have been delivered at an NRA convention, an organization embedded in a frame of fear: constructing a world in which agencies fail and the media is to be distrusted.

Focusing on warning signs and red flags undercuts the frame of needing to control guns: this frame suggests that if the mental health system is repaired and can deliver adequate services to those who are potentially violent, then there is no need to remove guns. Like so many themes above, there are substantial political differences in the use of this frame. Specifically, when comparing Republicans and Democrats, there are significant differences: whereas 6% of tweets of Republicans promote mental health reform (higher than would be expected), only 1% of tweets from Democrats do so (lower than would be expected).

A somewhat distinct theme in the mental health camp—about 2% of the sample—is that gun control would do more damage than good as it would distract the public from the need for mental health reform. A general user captures this idea quite succinctly:

> the utter lack of self-awareness re Marjory Stoneman students and their whining over clear backpacks is just . . . you can't make this up. welcome to the party, pals. How dare you punish us collectively over one crazy person? Yes, we're familiar with that too. #NRAMember

This tweet, which goes so far as to claim that students lack "self-awareness," posits that all gun owners are judged by the actions of one "crazy person," implying that guns shouldn't be regulated based on one individual's actions.

Thematically, these tweets reframe guns as a *solution*, such as one user who stated:

> The Leftist media doesn't want you to know about Will Pringle the Parkland Florida high school football player who says guns would have saved his coach's life.

With this tweet, the conversation about mental health and gun control comes full circle. Accordingly, tweets that speculate that gun control would only make killers more likely to attack, serve as a fitting example of a "counterclaim": statements that attempt to reframe socially accepted arguments (Gusfield, 1996). By emphasizing mental illness as the actual explanation for school shootings, the frame of guns as a potential *solution* comes to the fore. Surprising nobody, 23% of the tweets from the NRA argue this line of reasoning (compared to 2% of the sample more generally).

Despite its relative infrequency in this sample, the sentiment of focusing on mental health as what "went wrong" in this shooting still deserves discussion. A great deal of public attention has recently focused on mental health reform as the way to solve this problem. This has led to different modes of operating for teachers and school administrators, as evidenced by Eammon in the quote that headed this chapter. This real-world consequence is somewhat surprising, as tweets that promote mental health reform compose such a small percentage of the whole sample.

How can this be the case? Perhaps, Twitter does not accurately reflect the general view of society. More likely, however, is that elected officials, predominantly Republicans, promote mental health reform as the answer. And, given their political power at the time of the shooting, that messaging has trickled down to how major institutions such as schools and law enforcement agencies choose to go about making schools safer.

WHAT WORKS WHEN WE TALK ABOUT SCHOOL SHOOTINGS?

With these themes elucidated, the question remains as to what messages are the most effective in communicating with other users. To determine which messages best connect with the public, Table 4.3 presents the average "retweet" and "like" count for each of the major categories and their subsets, and indicates where these vary significantly from the overall average counts.

On average, a tweet in the sample received 140 retweets and 475 likes. There are only three themes that significantly differ from these numbers. First, tweets that simply report news stories are retweeted an average of 57 times and liked an average of 192 times, which is significantly less than average ($p < .001$). On its face this makes sense, as these tweets do not pack the same verbal punch as those promoting specific agendas. For individuals attempting to sway others' points of view and reach a larger number of people, one conclusion from this finding is that tweets that carry some form of opinion or statement of what should be done are more likely to be shared or retweeted than basic facts.

More notably, tweets that argue that mental health reform is the best way to solve the problem of school shootings are significantly undershared compared to the average (with 64 retweets and 166 likes on average). Numerically, in this public sphere the argument that mental illness led to the school shooting is less salient than the pro-gun-reform argument (which is not statistically different than the average). This is a curious finding, given the

Table 4.3. Average Retweets and Like Count by Category

Unrelated/News Stories	57.08***	Mental Health	165.55***
Mental Health	64.13***	Unrelated/News Stories	191.59***
Thoughts and Prayers	104.26	Thoughts and Prayers do NOT work	441.74
AVERAGE RETWEET COUNT	**139.88**	Gun Reform	466.74
Thoughts and Prayers do NOT work	144.78	**AVERAGE LIKE COUNT**	**474.55**
Support the Students	145.11	Thoughts and Prayers	509.23
Gun Reform	160.21	Support the Students	555.27
Stop School Violence Act	197.48	"Do Something"	719.91
"Do Something"	222.83	Stop School Violence Act	889.02
General Safety	239.39	The Police/School Failed	893.77
Gun Control is NOT the Solution	272.79	The Problem is Politicians	897.96*
The Problem is Politicians	300.86*	Gun Control is NOT the Solution	907.55
The Police/School Failed	304.68	General Safety	1100.15
The Students are Phony Actors	362.01	The Students are Phony Actors	1246.36
The Problem is the Media	364.93	The Problem is the Media	1391.14
Support Law Enforcement/ First Responders	371.44	Support Law Enforcement/ First Responders	1835.45
Ceremonies of Remembrance	515.3	Ceremonies of Remembrance	2431.6

*** p<.001; * p<.05, analysis conducted through t-tests, with retweet/like count of each category was compared to the retweet/like count of the sample mean.

seeming omnipresence of the "mental health" frame in popular discourse, by certain politicians, and in the minds of teachers today. On Twitter, that sort of rhetoric is not only rare but also rarely shared.

Lastly, the only tweets that lead to greater engagement by the general public are those that blame politicians for their failures. These tweets were retweeted about 300 times and liked about 900 times, significantly higher than average ($p < .001$). If Twitter accurately reflects the pulse of the public, this provides evidence that blaming politicians for their failings is both a widely used practice and a potentially useful tool for those interested in changing the conversation about school shootings.

IMPLICATIONS: WHAT DO WE DO NOW?

What we say about a situation *matters*. Words are not meaningless, as they are the building blocks of tangible actions (Snow et al., 1986). The way individuals frame a problem rhetorically has real-world ramifications in terms of public policy and resource allocation. In our modern reality where individual opinions can be shared online in seconds, the world of social media presents a particularly fruitful area for exploring how the public constructs frames: explaining social problems at warp speed. There are several points to emphasize that clarify this rhetoric's importance relating school shootings, gun control, and mental health.

First, the research herein showcases the general frames related to the Stoneman Douglas shooting in the Twitterverse: those of gun control, thoughts and prayers, supporting students, blaming institutions, and mental health reform. Though this research focuses on one event, the frames generated in this chapter provide readers, academics, activists, and other observers with a better understanding of what is being said publicly, what might be worth continued study, and what might be worth debunking in public forums. Future researchers should document other vocabularies of motive related to school shootings from previous school shootings, or (unfortunately) when the next one occurs.

Second, there is substantial variation in the use of these frames. Specifically, Democrats tend to promote gun control and support the students, whereas Republicans tend to provide thoughts and prayers and advocate for mental health. Congresspeople, particularly Democrats, blame politicians and an ineffective political process for not solving the problem more quickly, whereas other elected leaders, predominantly Republicans, laud the actions of first responders. Conservative news sources like Fox News and the NRA blame policing and media failings, while NPR and local news sources generally do not tweet out types of stories in ways that differ significantly from the general Twitter public at large. One can see how these groups view the world, which has notable outcomes for public discourse, teacher training, and what to "watch out for" when it comes to the life of our educators.

Third, the overwhelming focus on gun reform vs. mental health is notable. Tweets emphasizing the importance of mental health reform to solve the problem of school shootings are the rarest category tweeted, liked, or retweeted. Instead, this framing is used from the top-down, especially by politicians, who have staggeringly different views from the general public on the issue of school shootings.

While citizens call for legislative reform, elected officials, especially Republican ones, claim it's an issue of mental health. By focusing the conversation on delivering better mental health resources to our students, and shifting away from more stringent gun control, there is an increased burden for teachers, administrators, school staff, and students to be ever vigilant: in this world, it is not the imperative of legislators to make guns less accessible but for teachers to be on the lookout for signs of potential violence in their students. As one police agency tweeted:

> Please, if you #SeeSomethingSaySomething. Our thoughts and prayers are with #MarjoryStonemanDouglasHigh and #Parkland.

Teachers, fellow students, and administrators are presented with a reality where they must be on guard and exert constant vigilance with this sort of messaging: being told they should be doing more to identify potential shooters. This is emotionally and physically exhausting, and is not advocated by the vast majority of Twitter users in this sample.

Finally, when it comes to increasing engagement with Twitter users, the only messages that were retweeted and liked at higher rates than average are those related to political failings or that call out politicians for their inactivity or allegiance to pro-gun lobbyists. This was a tactic adopted early by the Parkland #MFOL team (Cullen, 2019), and one that future fighters for gun reform can use.

While this research cannot state what messages lead to actual reform, it makes clear what messages are shared and passed around in the Twitterverse. Because words have meaning in the way we construct our reality, activists can use this information to frame their arguments within the context of an ineffectual body politic: decrying the politicians in charge of moving legislation could be a stylistic and rhetorical choice to better convey their messages. This practice will not solve the issue of school shootings, but it is a step in the right direction to say #EnoughisEnough.

REFERENCES

Benford, R. D. (1997). An insider's critique of the social movement framing perspective. *Sociological Inquiry, 67*(4), 409–430.

Borah, P. (2011). Conceptual issues in framing theory: A systematic examination of a decade's literature. *Journal of Communication, 61*(2), 246–263.

Cullen, D. (2019). *Parkland: Birth of a movement*. HarperCollins.

Gusfield, J. R. (1996). *Contested meanings: The construction of alcohol problems*. University of Wisconsin Press.

Micalizzi, A. (2020). Exploring gender and sexuality through a Twitter lens: the digital framing effect of the #fertilityday campaign by female users. *Information, Communication & Society*, 1–18.

Mills, C. W. (1940). Situated actions and vocabularies of motive. *American Sociological Review, 5*(6), 904–913.

Pulido, C. M., Villarejo-Carballido, B., Redondo-Sama, G., & Gómez, A. (2020). COVID-19 infodemic: More retweets for science-based information on coronavirus than for false information. *International Sociology*, 1–20.

Snow, D. A., Rochford Jr., E. B., Worden, S. K., & Benford, R. D. (1986). Frame alignment processes, micromobilization, and movement participation. *American Sociological Review*, 464–481.

Spector, M., & Kitsuse, J. I. (2001). *Constructing social problems*. Transaction Publishers.

Twitter. (2020). About Twitter. htttps://about.twitter.com/

Chapter 5

Macabre Money: Capitalizing on School Shootings

Heather J. Matthews

"We've all been desensitized to the entire thing because you know, since we've been very young we've been doing it. They've always talked about it. It's not really new to anybody."—Liv, age 14

My awareness of the economics of school shootings came right after the Parkland school shooting, at Florida's Marjorie Stoneman Douglas High School, in 2018. I was a third-year teacher in a small rural school district in southern New York State. Many of my students worked on family farms, with the largest industry in the area being dairy and meat farming. I knew that my students were very familiar with guns, and I knew that most of them had shot at least one gun in their lifetimes—I have seen photo evidence of this fact, and heard many tales of turkey and deer hunting. I knew that most of my students had ready access to guns at their homes, and I had accepted this fact as just one of the many aspects of working at a rural school. I also knew that my district was objectively poor, as were many of the families who sent their children to the district.

The Parkland shooting was the first school shooting that received mass media coverage while I was teaching. Other school shootings had, of course, happened during my lifetime, but now that I was a teacher, I was now looking at school shootings not just as a tragedy, but as a danger to myself and my students. Suddenly, everyone wanted to talk about gun violence in schools: do we arm teachers, what can we expect of teachers, what are the protocols for keeping kids safe? I had more than a few nightmares about school shootings, and felt an impending sense of dread any time the school PA system rang out an unscheduled message.

The Parkland school shooting forced me to ask myself some difficult questions—could my students survive a two-story jump onto a paved parking lot if my classroom door was blocked? Where could I hide my twenty-five 7th grade students in a too-small classroom with no closets? Which items in my room could be used as shields, and which as weapons?

Thoughts like these rattled me so deeply that one afternoon, I found myself compelled to shop online for emergency escape ladders that would fit the brick work windows of my classroom, as well as a door security bar to impede entrance into my classroom. Eventually, this search led to my finding personal safety items, such as bulletproof backpacks, sweatshirts, and briefcases. I examined pages upon pages of bulletproof jackets and purse inserts, wondering if I should invest in such items.

My growing obsession with purchasing safety gear forced me to confront an aspect of school shooting that is not often talked about—the fact that there is an entire industry which builds wealth off of the fear and anxiety associated with shootings in schools. Every time that a teacher buys a door security bar, or a family buys a bulletproof backpack, someone is making a profit by selling that item. There are corporate entities who *need* my fear for their business model to thrive.

In fact, as of 2019, the appetite for school defense products has driven a $2.7 billion dollar industry (Cox & Rich, 2018; Everytown, 2020). This is a repugnant statistic that reflects the reality which families and school districts must grapple with. As 14-year-old Liv muses at the opening of this chapter, we are so desensitized to school shootings (and the need for personal protection against such shootings), that my looking at the dimensions and tensile strength of ballistic backpacks wasn't absurd, but just another aspect of my career. School shootings are seen more as an almost inevitable occurrence in many districts, and the only solution seems to be to throw thousands of dollars to preventative and reactionary measures, many of which may not even be useful or effective.

It's not only the production of safety gear that generates profit; school shootings are capitalized on in many forms: authors, screenwriters, musicians, businesses owners, and the media alike have found and will continue to find ways to profit from school shootings and the tragedies that follow. It is important to examine how the fear of gun violence in schools has evolved into a business model and to scrutinize exactly who benefits from it. Ultimately, the fact is that school shootings equal business opportunities, and the fear of death drives consumer behavior. Turning a profit on the backs of dead and wounded school children is, to put it mildly, macabre.

THE COST OF SCHOOL SAFETY

Newly popularized school safety conferences serve as one example of the growing industry generated by the fear of gun violence in schools. A simple Google search for the term "school safety conferences" will turn up pages upon pages of results showing conventions and conferences catering to parents, schools, school resource officers, and faculty alike, all over the world.

For the upcoming conference season, conventions for school safety make boasts such as describing themselves as, "the largest national school safety conference in the nation with over 1100 attendees & 125 exhibitors expected" (School Safety Advocacy Council, 2020, n.p.), and offer sessions in topics like, "Especially Safe: Planning & Preparing for the Safety of Students with Special Needs" (Safe and Sound Schools, 2020, n.p.). Many of these conferences feature speakers with military, law enforcement, or legal backgrounds, as opposed to pedagogical or administrative ones, and attendance for a multiday conference can cost upwards of $400 in registration fees alone (International School Safety Institute, 2020, n.p.).

One such convention, a 2018 expo for school security products, was held in Orlando, Florida. This expo boasted 105 vendors, selling school safety items such as "a 300-pound ballistic whiteboard—adorned with adorable animal illustrations and pocked with five bullet holes—that cost more than $2,900" (Cox & Rich, 2018, n.p.). Other items featured at this expo include "tourniquets and pepper-ball guns, facial-recognition software, and a security proposal that would turn former Special Operations officers into undercover teachers" (n.p.).

The steep price tag of any one of these items, let alone multiple items, is astronomical. One of the cheaper offerings at this expo, the aforementioned Special Operations undercover teacher's program would be equal to, "the price of a Netflix subscription" (Cox & Rich, 2018, n.p.) per family, per year, depending on school size. When comparing costs, the creator of a "high-tech, armored classroom door that, for the price of $4,000 [will] stop bullets, identify the weapon, photograph the shooter and notify police," had done the math for consumers—"if you think $500,000 [spent per year for a school safety system] is expensive, go down to Parkland, Florida, and tell 17 people $500,000 is expensive. That's $29,000 a kid. . . . Every person would pay $29,000 a kid to have their kid alive" (2018, n.p.).

This is flawed logic for many reasons; the foremost being that while every caring parent would pay an infinite sum to keep their child safe, fiscal reality impedes this desire. Many families would be unable to pay $29,000 per child, per year, on such a product. The vendor described above, and many others, prey on parents' natural desire to protect their children while hinting that failure to pay amounts to neglect.

Cox and Rich also add that proof that these items are effective is scant, writing that, "what few of the salespeople could offer, however, was proof [that these items work]" (2018, n.p.), suggesting that a family might, for example, subscribe to a $29,000 a year security plan in the hopes of keeping their child safe, and still become a victim of a school shooting.

As stated above, the school security industry "has grown into a $2.7 billion market—an estimate that does not account for the billions more spent on armed campus police officers" (Cox & Rich, 2018, n.p.). Efficacy aside, these systems are simply out of fiscal reach for many districts across the country.

Most teachers cannot afford a $2,900 whiteboard, especially knowing that they would probably not be reimbursed for such an item. Many families cannot afford to purchase a $150 bulletproof backpack (sold conveniently at Home Depot and Walmart, according to Cox and Rich), and to be frank, families should not have to consider purchasing a $150 bulletproof book bag for their child in order to feel that their child is truly safe at school. However, the implicit marketing message here is that any "good" parent or guardian will spend whatever amount of money required to ensure their child's safety, while in reality, only the wealthy could afford such a luxury.

Another school safety conference, the National School Safety Conference, held in Nevada in 2018, offered similar products and services. The National School Safety Conference offered for purchase such items as bullet-resistant blankets, flashlights with pepper spraying capabilities, and bullet-resistant backpacks and laptop cases (Campbell, 2018, n.p.). These items were priced at $1,995, $299, $500, and $800, respectively. Another item, unique to this conference, was a virtual staff training program titled Laser Shot. This training is structured as a video game, which requires teaching staff to target shoot in a virtual school library, where they find themselves facing down a teenage boy with a semi-automatic rifle (2018, n.p.). The price for this video game was not listed.

Of course, school shooting prevention and reaction products do not stop at doors and video game trainings—some districts have answered the call for increased school security with more expensive and drastic measures. A *Today Show* video from 2015, which featured the "safest school in America," shows off such school building modifications as bulletproof doors, live video feeds to a local sheriff office, staff member's ID lanyards equipped with panic buttons, and smoke cannons hidden within hallway ceilings.

In this program, a *Today Show* correspondent is walked through what a school shooting drill looks like, with children seated on the floor, holding textbooks in front of their faces to slow down bullets. At the end of the video, correspondent Jeff Rossen poignantly says, "Security does not come cheap.

That system, soup to nuts, costs $400,000 . . . but if schools can afford stadiums and uniforms, they can afford this" (Today.com, 2015, 3:53).

It is astonishing to see what it would take for a school building to be rendered "safe," and the enormous bill it would incur. Knowing the cost of a safety system, such as the one described above, one must question whether the average public school district could feasibly buy something comparable. How many stadiums could make up for these budget items? How many flutes, basketballs, or laptops would have to be sacrificed to cover the cost? How many rulers does a panic button cost? How many erasers equal a smoke cannon?

At its most extreme, some schools have been designed specifically to prepare for school shootings. As reported by WOOD TV8 (a Grand Rapids, MI, news source), one Michigan public school was being built for the purpose of keeping students safe in the event of an active shooter. This school, which will cost $50 million to build (according to Matt Slagle of Tower Pinkster, an architecture and engineering firm), brags of such features as "the ability to lock all doors from a smartphone (2019, 0:52), as well as "wing walls," which are meant to "help cut down on further line of sight of an active shooter . . . and provide students a place to hide" (2019, 0:57).

The building also features curved halls and large hallway-to-classroom bulletproof windows (WOOD TV8, 2019). In a time when public education is continually being defunded, a $50 million school building is unrealistic at best. Many school districts struggle to amass enough capital to keep academic and extracurricular programs funded, let alone to build what amounts to a high tech fortress.

Beyond the cost of physical infrastructure, school districts must also come up with funds to pay for professional development and training to prepare for what may seem to be inevitable incidences of gun violence. Teachers need to know whether their district agrees with the run-hide-fight model, or the avoid-barricade-counter-survive model, and what each step of the selected model entails. To help faculty and staff navigate school shooting preparation measures, many districts contract with local and national entities to provide yearly trainings. These trainings are often accompanied by pricey consultants, with districts footing a yearly bill to keep their faculty and staff updated in their training.

One such program, known as ALICE Active Shooter Response Training (which stands for alert, lockdown, inform, counter, evacuate) provides quotes upon request, but purportedly cost the Anchorage, Alaska, school district $56,000 for the 2016–2017 school year, plus "$25,000 in each of the next two years for training renewal" (Gajanan, 2016, n.p.), a price which has surely increased in the years since.

Beyond the cost of training programs are the legal fees incurred when that training goes bad; the National Education Association, the American Federation of Teachers union, and the Everytown for Gun Safety Support Fund all agree that school safety drills for active shooters can be damaging and traumatic for students and staff alike (Everytown, 2020, n.p.). The ALICE training drills, for example, have resulted in multiple court cases in which staff and students were injured both physically and psychologically, ending in out of court settlements with massive financial losses (O'Regan, 2019, n.p.).

Many districts do not have the capital to invest in sustained high-quality trainings for faculty and staff, let alone pay for any injuries, therapeutic measures, or leave-of-absences that can result from these trainings. According to O'Regan, the financial losses that districts suffer come from "emergency room bills for teachers and staff who are injured in [active shooter] drills," (2019, n.p.) as well as court case settlements for emotional trauma and PTSD suffered by faculty and staff (n.p.).

Other potential injuries and liabilities outlined in the ALICE waiver (which must be signed by all participants) include "minor injuries such as scratches, bruises and sprains; major injuries such as eye injuries, loss of sight, joint or back injuries, heart attacks and concussions," and, finally, "catastrophic injuries including paralysis and death" (2019, n.p.).

While the annual cost associated with the school safety training programs is rapidly increasing, some recent findings suggest that litigation and insurance costs due to injuries resulting from trainings is increasing even more. Active Threat Solution, which specializes in less traumatic trainings and drills, found that ERM Insurance Companies had, in less than two years, paid "more than a quarter-million dollars for emergency room bills of Iowa school employees who experienced active shooter training and were injured. These costs do not include follow-up doctor visits, physical therapy, surgeries or lost work time" (Active Threat Solutions, 2019, n.p.).

In their promotional materials, Active Threat Solutions describe the recent court case of an Oregon teacher who sued her district for "lost wages, medical costs and punitive damages," due to a diagnosis of PTSD caused by an active shooter training drill (n.p.). Safe Haven International supports these findings, stating that a Loss Prevention Education Manager for EMC Insurance Companies believed that if one company was suffering from such great losses in under 24 months, the national average of fiscal losses "are very likely in the millions" (Dorn, 2014, n.p.).

Dorn also states that many insurance companies are now classifying such active shooter trainings to be "high-risk activities" which will incur higher insurance premiums and fees (n.p.). It must be assumed that the school district, as well as faculty and staff, will ultimately pay these prices with their paychecks as well as with their bodies and minds.

Capitalizing on the fear of every parent that their child might die in an instance of school gun violence is disgraceful. However, corporate entities that exploit school shootings, who see death in school hallways as an opportunity, have coldly calculated the math. As the maker of the bulletproof blanket featured in the Nevada conference so succinctly stated, "It's cost versus value. The cost of [the blanket] versus the value of a life" (Campbell, 2018, n.p.).

No family or school district should be asked to calculate the cost of a child's or teacher's life. In impoverished districts, the math equation changes from shameful to impossible; the equation of cost versus value, where education at large is not valued enough to justify the cost of upgrades, and student mental health and emotional well-being are not valued enough to justify the cost of preventative measures. Ultimately, the cost of survival falls largely on families, who are then left to spend money in an effort to ensure their child's safety against the threat of an active shooter in school.

SCHOOL SHOOTINGS EN VOGUE

Beyond the world of school safety programs and products lies another, perhaps more insidious industry, attached to popular culture and entertainment, which benefits, albeit indirectly, from gun violence in schools. Weaponized school violence has its own fashion marketing niche, with clothing that can be purchased for everyday wear.

A trip to a local Walmart can land a customer an *American Horror Story* t-shirt featuring the face of popular character turned school shooter for the low price of $20.99 (Walmart, 2020). In 2019, the clothing brand Bstroy featured sweatshirts emblazoned with the names of infamous school shooting locations, complete with what appeared to be bullet holes, which the creators later stated was meant to be "ironic" and were meant to draw attention to the issue of school violence (Bates, 2019). The cost of these sweatshirts is unknown, as they were not brought to market; however, Bstroy sells typical sweatshirts at $550 each (Bstroy, 2020).

School shootings also turn a profit when featured in novels, television shows, movies, staged performances, and other popular art forms. Teens and adults alike read novels like *Nineteen Minutes* (Picoult, 2007), watch movies like *We Need to Talk About Kevin* (Ramsay, 2011), perform plays like *The Library* (Burns, 2014), and find many other ways to consume school shootings as entertainment. In recent years, there have been innumerable American and international television shows, books, movies, songs, and other forms of media which feature school shootings.

One could argue that using a school shooting as a plot device has become the new American zeitgeist, with writers feeling secure in the knowledge that employing such a plot device will ensure higher engagement, and subsequent sales, with consumers. One cannot assume to know whether these companies have created the desire for such items, or are simply supplying the public's demand, but it begs the question—why are these movies and t-shirts popular? There may be a multitude of reasons, but the implications are staggering; school shootings have become normalized aspects of our collective understanding of the experience of schooling, as the atrocities they are.

Some more recent examples of gun violence in media portrayals run the gamut in variety. One such example that can still be heard on popular radio stations is the song "Pumped Up Kicks," by the band Foster the People. Released in 2010, the lyrics tell the story of a boy named Robert who has found a gun in his father's closet; the chorus of the song is as follows: "All the other kids with the pumped up kicks / You'd better run, better run, outrun my gun. / All the other kids with the pumped up kicks / You'd better run, better run, faster than my bullet" (Foster the People, 2010).

While ambiguous about whether or not Robert actually becomes a school shooter or rather just fantasizes about the act, the lyrics are no mere coincidence. The band's front man, Mark Foster, has denied that the song is specifically about a school shooting, but has admitted that "Pumped Up Kicks" is about gun violence and his desire to bring awareness to such violent acts as school shootings (Zaru, 2017). The song was certified 6x platinum, selling over 5 million units (Newstead, 2014) before serving an altogether different purpose in 2018.

The gunman at the Parkland, Nikolas Cruz, reportedly had a connection to the song, both "urging people to listen to ["Pumped Up Kicks]" (Wetmore, 2019), as well as "strut[ting] around [his] house with a shotgun, playing ['Pumped Up Kicks'] and pretending to pull the trigger" (O'Matz, 2018). One cannot presume to know if this song was inspiration or simply a way for Cruz to act out his already set plans. The connection between "Pumped Up Kicks" and the Parkland shooter has largely led to the retirement of the song from the band's repertoire, though it has not quelled the song's popularity. Almost a decade after the original release of the song, it can still be heard on the radio, with new censorship layered over some provocative words (Zellner, 2019).

Another example of school shootings in recent media is the television show *Glee*, with the episode "Shooting Star." A long running television series which spanned six years, *Glee* focused on the glee club at an Ohio high school. Season four aired in 2013, with the season's 18th episode bearing the title "Shooting Star."

This episode of *Glee* deals with a potential school shooting as a plot device. In the episode, students at the high school hear two gun shots, and the audience watches their respective reactions—one student, stuck in the bathroom, is shown hiding her feet in a stall, crying, while other students are shown recording messages to their families in their phones in case they die (Murphy et al., 2013). Though ultimately, the gun firing is unrelated to an actual school shooting, the characters' agonized responses are realistic and familiar. However, the incident is not mentioned in later episodes, nor does the audience see any exploration of this traumatic event for any character beyond this episode.

Perhaps the most important fact regarding "Shooting Star" is not the plot point of the fired gun in a school building, but rather, the treatment of the topic and audience reactions. "Shooting Star" featured a content warning at the beginning of the episode, warning viewer discretion because the content would contain violence (Murphy et al., 2013). The episode aired only a few months after the 2012 Sandy Hook shooting in Connecticut.

Prior to airing, the Newtown Action organization's Facebook posted a message cautioning viewers about the episode's content; after airing, the producers were criticized for not alerting the Sandy Hook community before the episode aired (Carlson, 2013). Even so, "Shooting Star" had 6.8 million viewers who tuned in live for the episode as it aired, a higher viewership than average (Acuna, 2013), resulting in higher profits for 20th Century Fox, which produced the show.

One final sample of school shootings as fodder for entertainment can be found in a short-lived video game titled "Standoff." Originally titled "Active Shooter," "Standoff" was due for release on the gaming platform Steam in June 2018, mere months after the Parkland shooting (Lopez, 2018). The game featured a first-person shooter in which the player was either an active shooter in a school building, or a SWAT team member responding to it; if the player takes on the role of the active shooter, the objective is to kill as many other students as possible, using a wide variety of weaponry. Like many other first-person shooter games, "Standoff" had a death counter on screen, tallying the number of people killed.

However, "Standoff" was never released, due to massive public outcry from the Stoneman Douglas community, as well as from many other outraged constituencies. Bill Nelson, a Florida senator, even tweeted about "Standoff," stating that the game was "inexcusable" (Lopez, 2018, n.p.). Perhaps influencing Steam's decision to cancel the game, a Change.org petition demanding the cancellation of the game received more than 200,000 signatures (Robinett, 2018). An especially poignant line in the online petition reads as follows: "How can anyone sleep at night knowing that they are profiting from turning deadly school shootings into entertainment?" (2018, n.p.).

In addition to profit for individual creators, brand awareness has expanded too. For example, Foster the People was able to re-release "Pumped Up Kicks" on their first studio album, titled "Torches," due to the song's resurgent popularity. The status of "Pumped Up Kicks," and its radio play, as well as a very popular music video, would have helped bolster sales for both of the band's albums, as well as for sales of future Foster the People albums.

Likewise, perhaps due to the outcry from the *Glee* episode, creators were able to use their gained momentum to further not only *Glee*, but other projects. Interestingly, prior to filming "Shooting Star," Murphy, *Glee*'s creator and producer, was also a writer and producer for the television show *American Horror Story*. The first season of *American Horror Story* featured a school shooting plot line, a full two years prior to this specific *Glee* episode, which is now immortalized on Walmart t-shirts across the nation. Whether these portrayals in popular media serve to raise awareness, as Bstroy and Foster claimed to desire, or serve a darker purpose, the creators are sure to turn a profit.

DOLLARS AND SENSE

One proposed solution to school shootings, the purchasing of more guns and ammunition for arming school resource officers or even teachers, feeds another industry inescapably linked to the prevalence of school shootings—the firearms industry itself. *Newsweek* reported in 2018 that immediately following the Parkland shooting, firearms ammunition manufacturers saw a bump in their stock values (Persio, 2018). Looking back, *Newsweek* observed similar patterns after the Las Vegas massacre in 2017, as well as the Pulse Nightclub shooting of 2016 and the 2015 San Bernadino shootings (Kwong, 2017; Persio, 2018).

Cox and Rich found in their reporting on the 2018 School Safety Expo that spending on school resource officers following the Parkland shooting increased dramatically, despite the fact that in 19 years since the Columbine school shooting, only one incident has actually been stopped by an armed resource officer (2018, n.p.). Cox and Rich found that despite the common belief that the "mere presence of the officers may deter some gun violence," of the more than 225 school shootings since 1999, at least 40% of those schools employed an armed officer on the campus at the time of the shooting (2018, n.p.). In spite of these facts, manufacturers of guns and ammunition increasingly benefit from school shootings and other mass shootings, as crowds rush to purchase their goods without any proof that guns on school campuses can or will prevent future shootings.

The perpetuation of the trope that the "only thing that stops a bad guy with a gun is a good guy with a gun" is, in itself, false. In fact, as Newman et al. (2004) point out, gun ownership in the home actually increases the likelihood that a school shooting will occur, as they provide potential school shooters with access to guns. "The presence of guns [in the home] is clearly causally related to [school] shootings, but it is not clear that [guns] increasing availability accounts for the recent spate of massacres in schools" (2004, p. 70).

In essence, gun ownership does not predispose a student to become a school shooter, but all school shooters access guns somehow, and having such a weapon at home can provide an opportunity to commit armed violence. Ironically, it is possible that the increase in gun sales by adults purchasing them for their own personal protection has resulted in well-stocked arsenals just waiting for potential shooters to kill their classmates.

Though the correlation between school shootings and subsequent spending is strong and proven, there remains another, perhaps more important, connection between the economy and school shootings. That is, profit is not just an effect of school shootings, but also a cause. Research is beginning to show that school shootings are tied to socioeconomic factors in victimized communities.

A team of researchers from the Kellogg School of Management at Northwestern University have found that school shootings rose and fell with economic indicators, such as unemployment and foreclosure rates (Pah et al., 2017). The team isolated 535 incidences of school violence, and in order to discern which events be designated as school shootings, developed the following criteria: the incident must involve a gun being discharged, must involve students or school staff in some way, and must take place on the premises of a school campus. Of course, this eliminates instances of violence in which perpetrators attack with other weapons such as knives, or which take place off school property.

The researchers gathered data from 381 school shootings which occurred between 1990 and 2013, finding that the timing of these events were comorbid with the state of the economy in the communities in which they occurred. They noticed that between 1992–1994 and 2007–2013 elevated rates of school violence and were demonstrably tied to "economic distress" (Pah et al., 2017, p. 1).

In the communities under examination, financial insecurity, unemployment, and loss of prospects, led to feelings of lower self-esteem and lower self-control, which subsequently manifested in higher rates of drug and alcohol abuse, as well as an increase in violence. These results trickled down from the affected adult population into the lives of children who were exposed to the economic distress faced by their families.

This is not to suggest that the state of the economy is the sole indicator for predicting whether a shooting will or will not occur, or that other precipitating factors contribute, such as bullying and mental illness. However, there remains a link between communities or families in fiscal distress and the increase in likelihood of a school shooting. Pah and colleagues' research casts doubt on more commonly identified causes, for example, heavy metal music, violent video games, or a copycat behavior. Instead, their research shows that the state of the community at large is, in fact, one of the best predictors of an incident of gun violence in schools. Furthermore, this research points to the idea that those most affected by an economic downturn are also those most likely to become violent and take their feeling of helplessness and insecurity out on others.

As the authors of *Rampage: The Social Roots of School Shootings* allude, more fiscally attainable prevention measures have roots planted both physical and social infrastructure, such as fences around school yard perimeters, the introduction of a school resource officer, or the addition of social workers and counselors to schools (Newman et al., 2004), and it is undeniable that these factors make students, staff, and the community feel more safe, both physically and emotionally. However, these prevention efforts, much like the smoke cannon hallways or the bullet proof whiteboards, cost money that most districts simply do not have.

Other preventative measures, such as adopting zero-tolerance policies, are faulty at best and inappropriate at worst. They often disproportionately target students of color, students who benefit from services such as special education, or students who are enrolled in free and reduced lunch programs (Alnaim, 2018; Zweifler & De Beers, 2002). These social constructs can be drawn back to socioeconomic factors—without proper funding to alleviate economic disparity, social justice gaps, and mental health crises, students who feel hopeless and ignored may decide to take their frustrations out on their teachers and classmates.

CASHING IN ON COMPLACENCY

In 2019, Sandy Hook Promise produced a video titled "Back-to-School Essentials," which has, to date, been viewed over 6 million times, which focuses on back-to-school supplies, such as knee socks which can be used as tourniquets, or skateboards that can be used to break the glass of a window so that student can escape a classroom.

While this video does not actually focus on the literal consumerism of back-to-school shopping, Sandy Hook Promise's video connects the consumerism of back-to-school shopping with school safety with the follow message, "It's back to school time and you know what that means. School shootings are preventable when you know the signs" (Sandy Hook Promise, 2019, 0:58).

While tongue in cheek in delivery, the message is relevant—if a family cannot afford an item like a cell phone for a child to bring to school, the child cannot call or text for help, let alone to send a last message of love. Just as with bulletproof backpacks, parents and guardians are again confronted with the necessity of choosing to purchase items in an attempt to ensure their child's safety. While Sandy Hook Promise does not concern itself with issues of capitalism, the message that can be drawn is startling and apt; at what point do school supplies and school safety become one and the same?

School shootings and capitalism are entangled issues that cannot yet be separated—gun violence in schools can be linked to economic decline, and yet also linked to corporate profit. I may not know the solution to the problem of capitalizing on and monetizing school shootings but it seems that if there is a way to capitalize on a tragedy in America, some entrepreneurial individual will find a way to do so. I can say that the condemnation of businesses and products that cater to the school safety industry is not as simple as it is in theory.

By engaging in fear mongering, like using a bullet-ridden door as a prop to sell a protective one, enterprises that sell products and services associated with gun violence exploit the insecurities and fears of families, teachers, and schools alike. These businesses, and their owners, have a vested interest in school shootings. Of course, this is not to say that they condone school violence, nor revel in the fact; they are simply opportunistic. However, the fact remains that the fiscal reality of many families and school districts mean that school safety systems, products, trainings, and even buildings are often out of reach.

Returning to Liv's quote which opened this chapter, society cannot simply become complacent to the existence of shootings in our schools, nor to the fact that there is a profit motive lurking behind them. Society must not normalize the idea that safety can be purchased. Expecting gun violence in schools should never be accepted as inevitable. Only by carefully considering each dollar spent, and who in turn benefits from that sale can the system of capitalizing on school shootings be challenged.

I may have only been a middle school English teacher, but sitting in my classroom, weighing the cost of an escape ladder, I was struck by how a $200 purchase could mean the difference between life and death for myself and my students. I do not have a degree in economics, but I can follow the money.

We must recognize, however, that while capitalism deserves to be implicated for the part it plays in contributing to school violence, it can also be harnessed for good. The school safety industry thrives on the fact that school shootings occur with relative regularity in the United States. By voting for politicians who support school safety, student well-being, and gun control, and by voting for school budgets which support preventative measures as well as reactionary measures, capitalism can be used for the benefit of students.

It is not enough to pay out cash in hopes that gun violence we may be forced to encounter will be less deadly; money must be spent proactively. The businesses which benefit from gun violence in schools benefit due to the complacency of politicians and others in power, who are, in turn, numbed by their belief that school shootings will continue to occur. This does not need to be the future that students like Liv, or teachers like me, are faced with. Instead of asking schools to buy bulletproof doors, smoke cannons, and panic buttons, we must become proactive.

Reacting to school shootings, as opposed to seeking to understand the roots of this terrible problem, will only lead to more teachers like me, allotting their finances for ballistic purses, all while students become either desensitized or traumatized by active shooter drills. Soon enough, preparations for school shooting will become just another piece of the curriculum, as absurd as it sounds. This cycle of macabre money can be stopped; bulletproof backpacks do not need to be the new normal.

REFERENCES

Active Threat Solutions. (2019, March 28). Active shooter training in schools: What's going wrong? https://www.didactivethreat.com/blog/active-shooter-training-in-schools-whats-going-wrong

Acuna, K. (2013, April 12). There was a school shooting on "Glee" last night. *Business Insider.* https://www.businessinsider.com/glee-airs-school-shooting-2013-4

Alnaim, M. (2018). The impact of zero tolerance policy on children with disabilities. *World Journal of Education, 8*(1), 1–5. https://doi.org/10.5430/wje.v8n1p1

Bates, J. (2019, September 18). Streetwear fashion label BStroy designs hoodies with school shooting "Slogans." *Time.* https://time.com/5679058/bstroy-fashion-brand-mass-shooting-hoodies/

Bstroy. (2020). Shop. https://bstroy.us/collections/samsara

Burns, S. Z. (2014). *The library*. Dramatists Play Service, Inc.

Campbell, A. F. (2018, July 31). These 4 products say everything about America's gun problem. *Vox.* https://www.vox.com/2018/7/31/17514216/gun-violence-school-shootings-safety-products-gun-control

Carlson, E. (2013, April 12). "Glee" school shooting episode: Newtown anti-gun group says "Watch with caution." *Hollywood Reporter*. https://www.hollywoodreporter.com/live-feed/glee-school-shooting-episode-newtown-438646

Cox, J. C., & Rich, S. (2018, November 13). Armored school doors, bulletproof whiteboards and secret snipers. *The Washington Post*. https://www.washingtonpost.com/graphics/2018/ local/school-shootings-and-campus-safety-industry/

Dorn, M. (2014, September 3). Active shooter response training injury costs rapidly adding up. *Safe Havens International*. https://safehavensinternational.org/active-shooter-response-training-injury-costs-rapidly-adding/

Everytown. (2020, February 11). The impact of school safety drills for active shootings. Everytown Research & Policy. https://everytownresearch.org/report/the-impact-of-school-safety-drills-for-active-shootings/

Foster the People (2010). Pumped Up Kicks [song]. *On Foster the People*. Startime International.

Gajanan, M. (2016, August 28). Alaska's students will be taught to evade a school shooter. *Time*. https://time.com/4469968/alaskas-alice-student-school-shooter-evade/

International School Safety Institute. (2020). *Shaping the future of school safety symposium*. https://www.internationalschoolsafety.org/

Kwong, J. (2017, October 2). Gun stock shares surge after deadliest shooting in U.S. in Las Vegas, as has become typical after massacres. *Newsweek*. https://www.newsweek.com/las-vegas-shooting-sends-gun-stocks-soaring-675637

Lopez, G. (2018, May 29). A new video game simulated school shootings. After outcry, it got taken down. Vox. https://www.vox.com/2018/5/29/17405716/active-shooter-steam-valve-corp-video-game

Murphy, R., Falchuk, B., Brennan, I., Hodgson, M. (Writers) & Buecker, B. (Director). (2013, April 11). Shooting Star (Season 3, Episode 18) [TV series episode]. In Murphy, R., Falchuk, B., Di Loreto, D., Brennan, I., Friend, R., Lerner, G., Buecker, B. (Executive Producers), *Glee*. Fox Broadcasting Company.

Newman, K. S., Fox, C., Harding, D., Mehta, J., & Roth, W. (2004). *Rampage: The social roots of school shootings*. Basic Books.

Newstead, A. (2014, January 14). Foster the People announce album, drop new single. *Tone Deaf*. https://tonedeaf.thebrag.com/foster-the-people-announce-album-drop-new-single/

O'Matz, M. (2018, August 31). On Parkland shooter's playlist: "Pumped Up Kicks," a chart-topping song about school slayings. *Sun Sentinel*. https://www.sun-sentinel.com/local/broward/parkland/florida-school-shooting/fl-florida-school-shooting-pumped-up-kicks-20180828-story.html

O'Regan, S. V. (2019, December 13). The company behind America's scariest school shooter drills. *The Trace*. https://www.thetrace.org/2019/12/alice-active-shooter-training-school-safety/

Pah, A. R., Hagan, J., Jennings, A. L., Jain, A., Albrecht, K., Hockenberry, A. J., & Amaral, L. A. N. (2017). Economic insecurity and the rise in gun violence at US schools. *Nature Human Behavior*, *1*, 1–6.

Persio, S. L. (2018, February 15). Are gunmakers profiting from the Florida high school shooting? *Newsweek*. https://www.newsweek.com/do-gun-makers-make-money-mass-shootings-808258

Picoult, J. (2007). *Nineteen minutes*. Simon & Schuster.

Ramsay, L. (Director). (2011). *We need to talk about Kevin* [Film]. Oscilloscope Pictures.

Robinett, S. (2018). Valve—do not launch Active Shooter—a school shooter video game! Change.org. Https://www.change.org/p/valve-corporation-do-not-launch-active-shooter-a-school-shooter-video-game

Safe and Sound Schools. (2020). 2020 National Summit on School Safety. https://www.safeandsoundschools.org/events/national-summit-on-school-safety/

Sandy Hook Promise. (2019, September 17). *Back-to-school essentials | Sandy Hook Promise* [video]. YouTube. https://www.youtube.com/watch?v=b5ykNZl9mTQ

School Safety Advocacy Council. (2020). 2021 National School Safety Conference. https://schoolsafety911.org/schoolsafety/

Today.com. (2015, September 8). *Tour the "safest school in America,"* see its built-in smoke bombs [Video]. Today. https://www.today.com/video/tour-the-safest-school-in-america-see-its-built-in-smoke-bombs-520899139902

Walmart. (2020). *American Horror Story*—Tate—short sleeve shirt. Walmart.com. https://www.walmart.com/ip/American-Horror-Story-Tate-Short-Sleeve-Shirt-XXXXX-Large/677187549

Wetmore, B. (2019, December 5). Is it time to retire "Pumped up kicks"? Paper. https://www.papermag.com/pumped-up-kicks-retire-song-shootings-2641525276.html?rebelltitem=6#rebelltitem6

WOOD TV8. (2019, August 26). *New Fruitport High School designed with shooting in mind* [Video]. YouTube. https://www.youtube.com/watch?v=duD0zoj55zw

Zaru, D. (2017, November 3). Foster the People's Mark Foster talks "Pumped Up Kicks" and gun violence. CNN. https://www.cnn.com/2017/11/02/politics/foster-the-people-mark-foster-pumped-up-kicks-gun-violence/index.html

Zellner, X. (2019, December 4). Mark Foster on "Pumped Up Kicks" eight years later & why it's time to retire the song. *Billboard*. https://www.billboard.com/articles/columns/rock /8545337/ mark-foster-the-people-pumped-up-kicks-retire-interview

Zweifler, R., & De Beers, J. (2002). The children left behind: How zero tolerance impacts our most vulnerable youth. *Michigan Journal of Race and Law, 8*, 191–220.

Chapter 6

Sandy Hook Promise: Research Informed Practices

Rachel Masi and Justin E. Heinze

"Everyone wants to believe they could be the hero and save everyone, myself included. I am hopeful that I would be heroic in the face of terror, yet would I or any of my other classmates be willing to sacrifice everything we know and love to save each other?"—Aidan, age 16

PATHWAYS TO PROGRESS

Aidan, the young speaker in the selected quote above, should be deciding who to ask to prom, not who to save in the face of terror. Schools are safe places; however, rare instances of violent tragedy have generated reactionary efforts that are often unproven and lack evidence of effectiveness (Price & Khubchandani, 2019). By investing in research and partnerships, we have the opportunity to develop and promote effective and sustainable solutions to prevent school violence. Schools are an essential and appropriate place to provide universal prevention, intervention services, and create action (Anderson Moore et al., 2015).

Students, such as Aidan, need to be provided with the tools to feel empowered and safe, rather than at the mercy of unthinkable acts of violence. Approximately 95% of schools reported that students have been trained on emergency lockdown drills (Musu-Gillette et al., 2018); however, these types of tactics do not provide students with strategies to prevent violence before it happens (Moore-Petinak et al., 2020). Programs are needed more than ever to help students feel less alone and isolated, as well as to provide students with the tools to reach out to trusted adults when they or their friends need help.

Sandy Hook Promise (SHP) is a national nonprofit organization with the mission to end school shootings and create a culture change that prevents violence and other harmful acts that hurt children. SHP was created to respond to the need for safer schools and communities, working in partnership with University of Michigan (UM) to evaluate the Know the Signs programs for efficacy and reliability. This unique partnership is an illustrative example of the benefits and challenges to developing an evidence base for action through evaluation.

GRASSROOTS PROGRAMMING: SANDY HOOK PROMISE

Sandy Hook Promise (SHP) is led by several family members whose loved ones were killed in the tragic mass shooting at Sandy Hook Elementary School on December 14, 2012. SHP is a moderate, bipartisan organization that supports sensible policy solutions that address the human side of gun violence to make schools safer.

Supported by a grassroots movement of 5.3 million people nationwide, more than 12 million youth and adults have participated in Sandy Hook Promise's Know the Signs programs in more than 14,000 schools and youth organizations. SHP's Know the Signs prevention programs educate and empower youth and adults to recognize, intervene, and get help for individuals who may be socially isolated and/or at risk of hurting themselves or others. Through these no-cost programs, Sandy Hook Promise has averted countless school shooting plots, teen suicides, and other acts of violence.

SHP's programs provide a multitiered toward prevention and intervention. The organization's Know the Signs Programs include Start With Hello (SWH), Say Something, and the Say Something Anonymous Reporting System. Each program offers 30 to 40 minutes of student training that can be self-led or delivered by an SHP presenter, and include additional resource materials (lesson plans, activities, and discussion guides). These programs are supported by the formation of a Students Against Violence Everyone (SAVE) Promise Club to embed and sustain the programs' teachings and mission in the school community.

Prevention: Start with Hello

SWH is an age-appropriate prevention program that teaches youth in grades K–12 to minimize social isolation, empathize with others, and create a more inclusive and connected culture. Start With Hello Elementary is a digital program designed specifically for grades K–5 that includes an interactive storybook, short-form video series, games, and activities. Start With Hello Middle and High School is a program that educators can use to empower students to reach out and help others who may feel socially isolated and create a connected, inclusive school community.

Research has shown that programs and initiatives can help prevent aggressive and violent behaviors by enhancing connectedness, building healthy teacher-student relationships, providing access to mental and health services, and reducing poverty and violence in communities (Dodge et al., 2003; Foster et al., 2017; Ingram & London, 2015).

Early Intervention: Say Something and Say Something Anonymous Reporting System

Say Something (SS) is a violence early intervention and prevention education program that teaches youth and adults how to recognize warning signs and signals, especially on social media, of individuals who may be a threat to themselves or others and to "say something" before the person can hurt themselves or others.

The Say Something Anonymous Reporting System (SSARS) builds on the core SS program and includes a 24/7/365 anonymous reporting system via a downloadable app, telephone hotline, and website that students can use to report an issue when they see potential for violence or self-harm. These programs are available to all schools and funded through a mix of federal grants, grassroots donors, philanthropic partnerships, and the charitable giving of individuals to provide the trainings and resources at no cost to schools and youth organizations.

Research in violence prevention has found that often those who look to harm themselves or others communicate their plans or give some type of warning or indication prior to the event (Meloy & O'Toole, 2011; Silver et al., 2018; Vossekuil et al., 2002). The extensive research in the field provides evidence to suggest the importance of identifying, assessing, and intervening to reduce and prevent violence (National Threat Assessment Center, 2019).

MEASURING EFFECTIVENESS

There are a variety of programs available to school communities to address concerns in school safety. Therefore, it is important to develop a comprehensive strategy that meets the needs of the community, has the capacity to implement the program with fidelity, and includes a system to monitor and evaluate progress. Research has shown that multiple factors can impact the implementation of a program and the quality and intensity of implementation has significant influence on the outcomes of a program (Durlak & Dupre, 2008; Gottfredson & Gottfredson, 2001; Wilson et al., 2003).

As a first step in evaluating whether a program is right for a school, a needs assessment should be conducted to gauge whether the program will address the concerns of the community, and at what age students should be targeted to receive the most benefit. Needs assessments involve data gathering from stakeholders and can range from localized efforts (e.g., focus groups) to large, systematic surveys of community members.

In either case, the intent is to identify the problems facing school communities and available resources, as well as gain a better understanding of the context in which the program is operating. For example, if there is an increase in self-harm or bullying in 6th grade, a program that is implemented in 3rd–5th grade may be the best option to reduce those rates in 6th grade. Principals have reported that schools often undertake multiple prevention programs at one time, which can make high quality implementation difficult on an already overtaxed system (Gottfredson & Gottfredson, 2002). Therefore, it is essential that schools carefully select programs to address their concerns to have the maximum benefit.

An important complement to a needs assessment is the articulation and assessment of program theory (Grembowski, 2001). This process entails mapping the mechanism(s) by which the intervention will impact the problems identified in the needs assessment. Program theories are not necessarily complex or abstract; rather, they serve as the basis for a program's theory of change, which can often be described through a series of if-then statements.

If, for example, schools provide students with training to recognize signs that a peer is at risk to themselves or others, *then* those students will be empowered to inform a trusted adult. *If* students consistently report concerns to trusted adults, *then* actions can be taken and fewer violent events will occur. Program theories are frequently represented using a conceptual or logic model (Frechtling, 2007).

These visual representations of a program's theory of the cause and effect of the intervention are a convenient and accessible way to describe how programs will affect youth. They can also assist in generating consensus among stakeholders when considering evaluation objectives and questions. SHP worked with UM to develop a conceptual model that shows how Say Something/Start with Hello can reduce school violence by first improving school climate and interactions between students and adults. SHP shares this model along with program materials with potential schools to increase buy-in and participation.

Both the knowledge gained by assessing the needs of the school community to address safety and formal specification of program theory allows for greater engagement and critical buy-in from all stakeholders. At SHP, we have found that effective communication at each step promotes buy-in at all levels.

To this end, it is important to address three main areas of focus: (1) the concerns or needs in the community (2) the evidence and data that suggest this is the best approach to address those concerns (3) the participants and key stakeholders, and each of their roles in the program. Addressing each of these areas often and transparently will allow greater success in the long term by providing clear expectations, and engaging partners in the work.

Once a program has been selected and deemed appropriate to address the problems facing a particular school community, it is then important to evaluate the program's implementation, fidelity, and sustainability. Process-oriented evaluation is essential to support assertions that observed changes were the result of program activities and are equally informative when diagnosing why an expected change did not occur. Programs that had procedures monitoring implementation have shown to have a greater effect than those without monitoring procedures (Dubois et al., 2002).

Evaluating a program can be costly; however, it is important to measure how close to protocols (i.e. the procedures outlined by the developers) programs are able to be implemented, how effective they are at changing the desired outcome, and how they can be sustained over time without significant funding, and in the face of staff and student turnover. Evaluations can be done internally to measure a response to an intervention or they can be completed on a larger scale with a more rigorous research design.

Research has found programs which were evaluated and then implemented in collaboration with an outside research partner provided more training and supervision, and were found to be more effective than those that utilized internal practices alone (Wilson et al., 2003). Regardless of whether an external evaluator or internal capacity is utilized, developing a clear protocol describing program implementation is an effective method for recognizing and cataloging deviation in program delivery for identifying other concerns. Evaluation plans stemming directly from pre-established criteria in the protocol increase transparency and objectivity to external stakeholders.

In addition to careful documentation and monitoring of program implementation, research designs that govern data collection and observation can rule out competing explanations for attitudinal or behavioral change. Design approaches vary substantially in their scope, form, and function, but planning can increase confidence in the conclusions using relatively straightforward procedures (e.g., pre/post data collection; inclusion of a control group).

We have been able to develop rigorous research designs to measure the impact of our programs due to a strategic partnership with UM. Our study designs incorporate best practices from the social sciences that allow us to measure the impact of our programs on various outcomes in the school community relative to schools that did not receive programming. The studies have evaluated SHP's Know the Signs programs within two large districts across time periods at pre and post measures. These studies have evaluated student outcomes, school climate, and overall program fidelity and engagement.

The partnership with UM encourages a level of objectivity that might be challenging when an organization chooses to conduct a self-evaluation. At the same time, the UM evaluation objectives and plan are informed by repeated interactions with the SHP program staff, resulting in a more refined and deliberate set of outcomes that best suit the needs of the foundation or organization.

PARTNERSHIPS ARE ESSENTIAL TO GROWTH

Partnerships between nonprofits and private businesses have been a popular model to address social issues and build engagement. These relationships have been used by many nonprofits and businesses to build economic growth, recognition, and awareness (Shumate et al., 2018). In addition, for decades, research institutions have worked closely with community stakeholders and resources to conduct programmatic evaluations, identify public health concerns and barriers to service, and explore challenges to implementation (Drahota et al., 2016); however, there have been fewer examples of long lasting, and multisite partnerships between a nonprofit and academic or research institutions.

Research is a vital and necessary tool; however, it can be costly and time consuming. The demands of large-scale research evaluations can place tremendous burdens on a nonprofit. A partnership between a research institution and a nonprofit creates a symbiotic relationship in which the field of research can be advanced, while at the same time allowing a nonprofit to achieve greater impact and sustainability.

The unique partnership between Sandy Hook Promise and UM presents a model in best practices to create lasting and systemic change in school safety. Sandy Hook Promise provides first-hand knowledge, insight, access to community relationships and resources, while UM provides the tools for comprehensive, in-depth, objective and nonbiased research. An integrated team approach between the organizations has allowed for the balance of stakeholder interest, and an ability to play to our individual and collective strengths.

This partnership allows SHP to focus on direct service with the goal of saving lives and using research to create practical and important developments to the programs and overall mission. This model can be applied to universities and organizations looking to foster research and measure impact. Whether it is a university seeking a partner for research, a school seeking a partner to measure existing program delivery or assess their current needs, or an organization seeking a partner to assess and evaluate their programs, a partnership, such as this, can provide objective insight and effective solutions.

GATHERING EVIDENCE TO DETERMINE BEST PRACTICES

UM and SHP have conducted two comprehensive research studies to evaluate the Know the Signs Programs. These studies—a nonequivalent, control group design in Los Angeles Unified School District (LAUSD) and a cluster-randomized control trial (i.e., where schools are randomly assigned to receive the program or not) in Miami-Dade County School District—compare students attending schools exposed to Knows the Signs programming to students attending matched control schools not exposed to the programming.

LAUSD, 2016–2017

The partnership began with an evaluation of Know the Signs conducted in LAUSD in the 2016–2017 school year with UM leading the research. We used a combination of self-report teacher and student surveys, qualitative interviews, and school administrative data to assess the program outcomes. Twenty-one schools participated in the study, with 1,555 middle and high school students completing surveys. Ten schools participated as treatment sites and received the Know the Signs programming while the remaining eleven schools operated normally. Data collected from teachers and students in both groups of schools were compared on socioemotional outcomes following the end of the program period.

The findings provided preliminary support for the efficacy of Know the Signs in improving attitudes toward school and risk behavior with small to moderate differences in the attitudes or behaviors of students who received Know the Signs versus those who did not. Participating youth reported significant improvement in attitudes towards taking action to prevent violence, reporting warning signs, and perceptions of school safety.

Program attendees also had higher perceptions of school safety and positive attitudes toward school as well as *fewer aggressive behaviors* compared to youth that did not receive the program. Several features of the study design qualify these results, including truncated program implementation, sample attrition at follow-up, and nonrandom assignment of schools to condition.

Miami, 2018–2020

In an effort to replicate and extend the findings from the LAUSD effort, SHP and the UM research team evaluated the addition of the Say Something Anonymous Reporting System (SSARS), an "all-in-one" application on computers, phones, and tablets developed by SHP that allows anonymous submissions of tips via multiple mediums when sharing concerns with trusted adults is not an option. The SSARS is paired with the SS curriculum emphasizing positive change of school climate, through educational training and student engagement.

The study design utilized a 2-group randomized control experimental design with 29 middle and high schools (n = 14 control, n = 15 intervention) and more than 1,000 students in the Miami-Dade County School District. An important characteristic of this design was that schools were randomly selected to either receive Know the Signs or not. Because assignment was random, there is more confidence that the two groups of schools were equal at the start of the study and that any subsequent differences observed were because of Know the Signs exposure and not some feature of the participating schools (e.g., size; student composition).

As in LAUSD, we used multiple methods to collect data to assess school climate, risk reporting, incidents and school-community response including: pre- and post-test surveys with students, teachers and school administrators, data extraction from ARS and school and police administrative records, and semistructured interviews with key school personnel.

Preliminary results from each study contributed to ongoing support that has enabled more nuanced study of Know the Signs programs with increasing rigor in the approach. The interactive relationship of our partnerships encourages the reciprocal sharing of data, which both inform SHP programming practice and the study team approaches to building evidence in support of Know the Signs.

RECOMMENDATIONS FOR FUNDING, TRAINING AND TECHNICAL ASSISTANCE, AND ENGAGEMENT

Based on the above findings and research, we have made several recommendations to promote the fields of education and public health research and save lives through education, prevention, and early intervention. These recommendations address three major areas of concern: funding, training and technical assistance, and engagement.

Funding

Funding Firearm Research

Overall, there needs to be an increase in funding for research on gun violence prevention and school safety. For decades, research and messaging has focused on firearm policies and safety, cost to society, and individual characteristics of perpetrators and victims. Thus, providing only a limited lens and lack of extensive research on gun violence prevention.

The restricted scope of research is due in part to the Dickey Amendment, passed in 1996, which restricted the CDC from conducting research on gun violence. The Dickey amendment stated that "none of the funds made available for injury prevention and control at the Centers for Disease Control and Prevention (CDC) may be used to advocate or promote gun control" (104th Congress. Public Law 104–208). It was then repealed in 2013 by the Obama administration; however, in 2012 and 2013 Congress blocked 10 million in funding for CDC'S gun violence research.

Compared to other areas of public health research, there has been minimal research on gun violence prevention (Stark & Shah, 2017; Rosenberg et al., 2017). Gun violence is substantially underfunded and underresearched when compared to other leading causes of death with similarly high mortality rates (Stark & Shah, 2017).

The research conducted by UM with SHP would not have been feasible without federal and private funding. Funding needs to be more accessible for prevention and intervention research. The inability to conduct comprehensive research on gun violence compromises our knowledge and recognition of the impact of specific gun violence prevention programs and policies. For example, despite homicide being the number one contributor to potential years of lost life among Black Americans there has been minimal public funding allocated to homicide research (Rosenberg et al., 2017).

Research on gun violence and school safety has the potential to identify and explore promising gun violence prevention policies. For example, a recent study found that looking across 45 years of policies that handgun waiting periods significantly reduce gun deaths by homicide and suicide (Luca et al., 2017). Research on gun violence can illuminate a problem, identify key solutions, and evaluate effectiveness in an effort to save lives.

The limited funding allocated to firearm research relative to other risks with similar youth injury burdens (e.g., motor vehicle crashes; cancer) (Cunningham et al., 2018) underscores the need to consider efficiency (i.e., cost/benefit) as part of evaluation efforts. Typically reserved for more established efforts and evidenced-based approaches, efficiency evaluations consider questions related to relative impact when resources are limited or scarce.

For many school communities, investments in large-scale prevention efforts are infeasible or face resistance from stakeholders given the burden on financial and human capital. Administrators can point to efficiency results to quantify return on investment or cost effectiveness ratio and argue for the continuation or redirection of their prevention efforts (Zhou et al., 2014).

Cost-saving measures from program developers should be communicated and tested, as well. For example, SHP offers a virtual program delivery that allows for greater reach at lower cost without sacrificing effectiveness. Incorporating efficiency assessment as a component of firearm prevention evaluation efforts can guide others considering implementing programs and determining fit for a school's or district's available resources and capacity.

Funding Programs and Practices

In addition, federal and state policies should provide funding for programs, as well as research, to promote avenues to success. Policies and resources such as the Students, Teachers, Officers Preventing (STOP) School Violence Grants Program (OMB No. 1121-0329), and the National Center for School Safety funded through the Bureau of Justice Assistance, and the Office of Community Oriented Policing Services (COPS) provided necessary funding and tools for schools to implement programs on school safety.

These policies and initiatives allow schools and communities to find evidence based practices that best suit the needs of their school communities and, with appropriate funding, implement them with fidelity, thus increasing the probability for success and long-term effects. STOP and COPS funding help SHP provide program training, materials, and support to schools at no cost. Without these crucial funding streams, schools often have to rely on their own blended funding streams to support prevention programs. Comprehensive funding plans are needed to create systemic and lasting change in the field of school safety and prevention.

Training and Technical Assistance

Training and technical assistance provide support to school communities in a variety of ways. A multidisciplinary team can create a holistic approach, and train individuals in school safety with a trauma-informed prevention lens. Practitioners in the school community, from the school resource officer to the principal on multidisciplinary teams should be trained to understand and implement the best practices in the field of prevention.

A technical assistance center provides resources for teams and individuals to learn skills to promote school safety, and access funding. Technical assistance can help provide information on grant writing, funding streams, and best practices for schools to be well informed in their approach to school safety (Durlak & DuPre, 2008).

Training students and teachers to recognize the signs of violence, and the steps to take to get help to prevent the violence to self or others is a critical line of defense in violence prevention. A report on Chicago Public schools cites that school violence often begins and escalates on social media between students (University of Chicago, 2019), and research has shown that children who self-harm are more likely to tell a peer and seek help from a friend rather than an adult (Evans et al., 2005).

We need to train students like Aidan, the student whose quote unfortunately captures the all too common experience of our students, to look for warning signs and to take action. This will empower students like Aidan, sustain safety measures, and help create a safe school community.

Programs that train and educate students, staff, and communities can strengthen these systems to reduce risk factors for violence and enhance protective factors to decrease the likelihood of violence and mental duress. SHP offers educators and parents trainings in suicide prevention and how to be a trusted adult for students to ask for help or report concerns. These trainings also include resources with additional information on these topics.

Training related to violence prevention cannot end at school boundaries; messages need to be reiterated at home and in students' neighborhoods. Training and technical assistance for parents and community members related to gun violence prevention is an understudied approach that could have important ramifications for the success of programs within schools.

Similarly, as students spend increasing time engaging in virtual interactions, considering how such messages are transmitted and reinforced in virtual spaces is a burgeoning area of research and practice. Programs and initiatives can help prevent aggressive and violent behaviors by enhancing connectedness, building healthy teacher-student relationships, providing access to mental and health services, and reducing poverty and violence in communities.

Engaging Schools to Create Sustainable Solutions

Engagement in community-based programs to promote healthy and safe communities can reduce tragedies through education, prevention, and intervention. A positive school climate, healthy relationships, and individual well-being can foster and promote a collaborative and safe environment to raise awareness, increase recognition, and create action.

A multitiered, which allows schools and professionals to intervene at the appropriate level of need, is shown to be imperative in identifying and implementing successful interventions. Research has shown that SHP engagement of students and staff is an effective and important element to program success.

SHP is a model for developing programs to meet the needs of students and school communities. SHP has been able to adapt to changes in education, and expand their reach by providing program delivery options, such as self-led, in person, online and/or digital formats. SHP's inclusion of SAVE Promise Clubs and available guides and resources has created a sustainable culture in schools long after a training presentation has been made.

In addition, SHP continues to align their programs with the Collaborative for Academic, Social, Emotional Learning (CASEL) and competencies for Social-Emotional Learning (SEL). This has been an important step towards engaging schools in their commitment to prevent youth violence, and improve school climate. By embedding these crucial SEL skills, schools are able to participate in the programming despite the common barrier of limited time allotted during the school day, and students gain these essential skills for their growth and well-being.

Unfortunately, schools often rely on programs or initiatives that have very little evidence or support. These programs can be costly, time consuming, and at times ineffective. The challenges and barriers to acquiring adequate funding make it difficult to evaluate programs and practices to inform schools' decisions. Investing time and funding in the critical work of program evaluation and implementation can have a direct impact on students' safety. Forming creative partnerships between public, private, and nonprofit sectors can help fill this gap in the field of school violence prevention to reduce school violence, promote safe and healthy communities, and protect and empower students like Aidan.

REFERENCES

Anderson Moore, K., Stratford, B., Caal, S., Hanson, S., Hickman, S., Temkin, D., Schmitz, H., Thompson, J., Horton, & S., Shaw, A. (2015). *Preventing violence: Understanding and addressing determinants of youth violence in the United States*. Child Trends.

Cunningham, R. M., Walton, M. A., & Carter, P. M. (2018). The major causes of death in children and adolescents in the United States. *New England Journal of Medicine, 379*(25), 2468–2475.

Dodge, K. A., Lansford, J. E., Burks, V. S., Bates, J. E., Pettit, G. S., Fontaine, R., & Price, J. M. (2003). Peer rejection and social information–processing factors in the development of aggressive behavior problems in children. *Child Development, 74*(2), 374–393.

Drahota, A., Meza, R. D., Brikho, B., Naaf, M., Estabillo, J. A., Gomez, E. D., Vejnoska, S., Dufek, S., Stahmer, A. C., & Aarons, G. A. (2016). Community-academic partnerships: A systematic review of the state of the literature and recommendations for future research. *The Milbank Quarterly, 94*(1), 163–214.

DuBois, D. L., Holloway, B. E., Valentine, J. C., & Cooper, H. (2002). Effectiveness of mentoring programs for youth: A meta-analytic review. *American Journal of Community Psychology, 30*(2), 157–197.

Durlak, J. A., & DuPre, E. P. (2008). Implementation matters: A review of research on the influence of implementation on program outcomes and the factors affecting implementation. *American Journal of Community Psychology, 41*(3–4), 327.

Evans, E., Hawton, K., & Rodham, K. (2005). In what ways are adolescents who engage in self-harm or experience thoughts of self-harm different in terms of help-seeking, communication and coping strategies? *Journal of Adolescence, 28*(4), 573–587.

Foster, C. E., Horwitz, A., Thomas, A., Opperman, K., Gipson, P., Burnside, A., Stone, D. M., & King, C. A. (2017). Connectedness to family, school, peers, and community in socially vulnerable adolescents. *Children and Youth Services Review, 81*, 321–331.

Frechtling, J. A. (2007). *Logic modeling methods in program evaluation* (Vol. 5). John Wiley & Sons.

Gottfredson, D. C., & Gottfredson, G. D. (2002). Quality of school-based prevention programs: Results from a national survey. *Journal of Research in Crime and Delinquency, 39*(1), 3–35.

Gottfredson, G. D., & Gottfredson, D. C. (2001). What schools do to prevent problem behavior and promote safe environments. *Journal of Educational and Psychological Consultation, 12*(4), 313–344.

Grembowski, D. (2001). *The practice of health program evaluation*. Sage Publications.

Ingram, D., & London, R. (2015). The Health Consequences of Social Isolation: "It Hurts More Than You Think." Beyond Differences. http://beyonddifferences.org/media/uploads/teacherdocs/consequences_of_social_isolation_2015-2016.pdf.

Luca, M., Malhotra, D., & Poliquin, C. (2017). Handgun waiting periods reduce gun deaths. *Proceedings of the National Academy of Sciences, 114*(46), 12162–12165.

Meloy, J. R., & O'Toole, M. E. (2011). The concept of leakage in threat assessment. *Behavioral Sciences & the Law, 29*(4), 513–527.

Moore-Petinak, N., Waselewski, M., Patterson, B. A., & Chang, T. (2020). Active Shooter Drills in the United States: A National Study of Youth Experiences and Perceptions. *The Journal of Adolescent Health: Official Publication of the Society for Adolescent Medicine, 67*(4), 509–513.

Musu Gillette, L., Zhang, A., Wang, K., Zhang, J., Kemp, J., Diliberti, M., and Oudekerk, B. A. (2018). Indicators of School Crime and Safety: 2017 (NCES 2018-036/NCJ 251413). National Center for Education Statistics, U.S. Department of Education, and Bureau of Justice Statistics, Office of Justice Programs, U.S. Department of Justice.

National Threat Assessment Center. (2019). Protecting America's schools: A US Secret Service analysis of targeted school violence. https://www.secretservice.gov/data/protection/ntac/usss-analysis-of-targeted-school-violence.pdf.

Price, J. H., & Khubchandani, J. (2019). School firearm violence prevention practices and policies: functional or folly? *Violence and Gender, 6*(3), 154–167.

Rosenberg, M., Ranapurwala, S. I., Townes, A., & Bengtson, A. M. (2017). Do black lives matter in public health research and training? *PloS one, 12*(10), 1–12.

Shumate, M., Hsieh, Y. P., & O'Connor, A. (2018). A nonprofit perspective on business–nonprofit partnerships: Extending the symbiotic sustainability model. *Business & Society, 57*(7), 1337–1373.

Silver, J., Simons, A., & Craun, S. (2018). A study of the pre-attack behaviors of active shooters in the United States between 2000 and 2013. Federal Bureau of Investigation, U.S. Department of Justice, Washington, D.C. 20535

Stark, D. E., & Shah, N. H. (2017). Funding and publication of research on gun violence and other leading causes of death. *Jama, 317*(1), 84–85.

University of Chicago, & United States of America. (2019). Connect and Redirect to Respect.

Vossekuil, B., Fein, R. A., Reddy, M., Borum, R., & Modzeleski, W. (2002). *The final report and findings of the Safe School Initiative*. Washington, DC: US Secret Service and Department of Education.

Wilson, S. J., Lipsey, M. W., & Derzon, J. H. (2003). The effects of school-based intervention programs on aggressive behavior: A meta-analysis. *Journal of Consulting and Clinical Psychology, 71*(1), 136.

Zhou, F., Shefer, A., Wenger, J., Messonnier, M., Wang, L. Y., Lopez, A., Moore, M., Murphy, T.V., Cortese, M., & Rodewald, L. (2014). Economic evaluation of the routine childhood immunization program in the United States, 2009. *Pediatrics, 133*(4), 577–585.

About the Editors and Contributors

Kjersti VanSlyke-Briggs is a Professor of Secondary Education and Educational Technologies at the State University of New York, Oneonta. She was the inaugural director of the Faculty Center for Professional Development of SUNY Oneonta and has now returned to the classroom. She is a past President of the New York State English Council (NYSEC) and was the editor of the journal *The English Record* during her time with NYSEC. Her primary research interests are in the intersection of literacy and social media as well as young adult literature (YAL). She is the author of *The Nurturing Teacher* and a coeditor of *Resisting Reform: Reclaiming Public Education through Grassroots Activism*. Her work in the last three years was focused on school shootings and media including in YAL. She received her doctorate from Binghamton University.

Elizabeth A. Bloom is a Professor of Education, Chair and Accreditation Coordinator of the Education Program at Hartwick College in Oneonta, New York. She is the past President of the New York State Foundations of Education Association (NYSFEA) and a founding board member of Move Up Global, an organization dedicated to bringing education and health to resource-constrained rural communities in Rwanda. Her research and advocacy interests align in the areas of education policy and history education. She is a coeditor of *Resisting Reform: Reclaiming Public Education through Grassroots Activism*. She received her doctorate from Binghamton University.

* * *

Fatima Albrehi is a doctoral student of communication and instructor at Wayne State University in Detroit, MI. Her research interests center on interpersonal ostracism, hip hop culture, and ostracism of marginalized groups by dominant groups. She approaches much of her research from an intercultural lens.

Ryan Ceresola is an Assistant Professor of Sociology at Hartwick College. His research and teaching interests include analyzing public sentiment on Twitter, white-collar crime, political corruption, and the implications of conspiracy theories in modern times. His work has appeared in *Crime, Law, and Social Change; Qualitative Sociology Review;* and *Sociological Perspectives.*

Justin E. Heinze is an Educational Psychologist and Assistant Professor at the University of Michigan School of Public Health. His research investigates how schools influence disparities in violence and other risk outcomes from an ecological perspective that includes individual, interpersonal, and contextual influences on development. He is a director of the National Center for School Safety, a training and technical assistance provider for schools implementing safety and health promotion programming.

Gina L. Keel is Professor of Political Science at the State University of New York, Oneonta. She conducts research and writes about public policy. She has contributed book chapters and articles to *Food Labeling Politics and Policy in the United States* (2020), *First Amendment Studies* (2014), *Governing America* (2010), *Encyclopedia of the U.S. Government and the Environment* (2011). She earned a BA in Political Economy of Industrial Societies from University of California, Berkeley, and a PhD in Politics from Brandeis University.

Brian M. Lowe is a Professor of Sociology at the State University of New York, Oneonta. He is author of *Emerging Moral Vocabularies: The Creation and Establishment of New Forms of Moral and Ethical Meanings* (Lexington, 2006) and *Moral Claims in the Age of Spectacles: Shaping the Social Imaginary* (Palgrave Macmillan, 2017).

Rachel Masi is the Director of Research at Sandy Hook Promise and a licensed clinical psychologist with a private practice. At Sandy Hook Promise, she oversees research evaluation studies and utilizes the findings to improve program development. She specializes in education, child and adolescent development, and clinical psychology.

Heather J. Matthews is a doctoral student at the University of Tennessee, Knoxville. She specializes in children's and young adult literature, with a focus on diverse racial and ethnic representations. Previously, she was a K–12 literacy specialist in New York.

Lukas Pelliccio is an Assistant Professor of Mass Communication at Lincoln University of PA. He received his PhD in Communication from Wayne State University. He has studied the interpersonal communication of ostracism for over a decade and is active in the communications discipline as an administrator, reviewer, and presenter for various communication organizations and conferences.

Armando Velazquez Jr. is a third-year Art and Business Double Major at Hartwick College in Oneonta. His focus is Graphic Design and Illustration. After he graduates, he hopes to design at major firms combining the skills he's acquired from both of his majors. Armando created the cover art for *A Relentless Threat: Scholars Respond to Teens on Weaponized School Violence* and *Dress Rehearsals for Gun Violence: Confronting Trauma & Anxiety in America's Schools.*